Keep following Jesus

Pastor

Dale

MORE THAN A BELIEF

Daily Devotions for Following Jesus

DALE SATRUM

WESTBOW
PRESS®
A DIVISION OF THOMAS NELSON
& ZONDERVAN

THE HOLY BIBLE, NEW INTERNATIONAL VERSION®, NIV® Copyright © 1973,
1978, 1984, 2011 by Biblica, Inc.® Used by permission. All rights reserved worldwide.

All Scripture quotations, unless otherwise indicated, are taken from the Holy Bible, New
International Version®, NIV®. Copyright ©1973, 1978, 1984, 2011 by Biblica, Inc.™
Used by permission of Zondervan. All rights reserved worldwide. www.zondervan.com

WestBow Press books may be ordered through booksellers or by contacting:

WestBow Press
A Division of Thomas Nelson & Zondervan
1663 Liberty Drive
Bloomington, IN 47403
www.westbowpress.com
1 (866) 928-1240

ISBN: 978-1-5127-6835-0 (sc)
ISBN: 978-1-5127-6836-7 (hc)
ISBN: 978-1-5127-6834-3 (e)

Library of Congress Control Number: 2016920757

Print information available on the last page.

WestBow Press rev. date: 01/04/2017

CONTENTS

DEDICATION

More Than a Belief is dedicated to my best friend and wife, Lisa, who has been following Jesus with me, side by side through the chaos and calm of life, for over thirty years. You are the best traveling partner I could have ever asked for.

To my two daughters, Rachael and Jessica, who are now following Jesus in their own families. I am so thankful that being PKs didn't hinder you but rather helped you follow Jesus as adults. I am very proud of you both.

To my church family at Foothills Community Church. Thank you for not just believing in Jesus. Thank you for the extreme privilege of following Jesus together on the greatest adventure ever.

FOREWORD

You are invited to join my pastor and me as we continue our journey in discovering what it means to "follow Jesus." We are on a practical pathway that is helping us understand how Jesus wants to use the experiences we encounter in life to help us grow spiritually and get to know Him better. He wants to use His word to align our hearts with the heart of God.

In *More Than a Belief,* Pastor Dale has provided an avenue to help you grow spiritually and experience a closer relationship with Jesus. *More Than a Belief* will benefit you the most if you take the following steps:

- Surrender your will to God.
- Give Him the right of way. Say yes in advance to every part of your life.
- Let Jesus be *your* shepherd. Trust Him to lead you in the paths of righteousness to green pastures and quiet waters.
- Always keep His sandals in view. He declared, "I am the way, the truth and the life." (John 14.6)
- Give your heart to God every day—not just part of your heart but all of it.

Following Jesus will fulfill your deepest and greatest longing. That's what my pastor and I are doing. We're doing our best to follow Jesus.

As you spend time in *More Than a Belief*, you will see your relationship with Him in a new light; God will touch you in a fresh way. You will develop a "want to" that will help you choose to spend quality time alone with God consistently. When you carve out your time to meet with God, record what you hear from Him and respond in prayer.

My relationship with Pastor Dale began in 1980 when I became his youth pastor. Now he is my pastor, my favorite pastor, and my friend. He is dearly loved and highly respected in the church and in the community as a man after God's own heart.

Pastor Dale is a visionary leader who hears from God and isn't afraid to step out in faith with the courage to follow Jesus, even when the next step takes him into uncharted waters. He is a man who believes his highest calling is to be a follower of Jesus—to exemplify Jesus in his family, church, and community. He desires the same for us, and that's why he wrote *More Than a Belief* for you.

Pastor Dale puts it this way. The scripture says, "Taste and see that the Lord is good...." (Ps. 34:8)

Pastor Dave Halbert
Mentor and friend

ACKNOWLEDGMENTS

I want to thank all those who helped this book become a reality. It was such a collaborative effort.

- Thank you, Julie Monroe-Falk, for your tireless effort at editing and refining this project. Thank you for being the point person for WestBow. If I'd had to do all the fine-tuning and meticulous detail myself, this book would still be just an idea. You have been amazing.
- Thank you, Lizz Kline, for the cover art and creative design.
- Thank you, Karen Willcut, for your creative input.
- Thank you, Sam Stuckey, for driving the creative process with the cover. It looks cool because of you.
- Thank you, Sandy Kundert, for being the grammar police and being another set of eyes with the editing.

INTRODUCTION

Matthew 4:19 says, "'Come, follow me,' Jesus said."

Jesus called people to *follow* Him, not simply *believe* in Him. Over the years it seems that Christianity has become synonymous with merely a specific belief system. If we agree to this way of believing, this makes us "Christians." We have focused on believing instead of following. Now we have created a version of Christianity that is nothing like what Jesus taught. We have diminished what Jesus said into a simple set of beliefs instead of a radically different lifestyle, a lifestyle of following Him.

The distinguishing trait of those of us who confess a faith in Jesus is that our belief so profoundly impacts us that it alters our very lives. We choose to follow Someone other than ourselves. This Someone is the living Jesus, our resurrected Savior, the One who is still speaking, still calling, and still leading His people today.

Jesus has never stopped calling people to follow Him. He is still calling you. He is still calling me. The wonderful thing is that you and I can learn to hear His voice and follow His leading. We can move from merely a set of beliefs to a living, breathing relationship with Jesus, where He leads us through the chaos and confusion of this life.

This process will take some time. It is going to require some effort. It won't always be easy. It doesn't "just happen." The journey, however, is worth taking. This devotional is simply a tool to help you learn, grow, reflect, and experience what following Jesus looks like. Here are some final thoughts before you can begin to succeed in this journey:

- Decide on a specific time to read and reflect every day.
- Tell someone else about your decision to make yourself accountable.
- If you miss a day or more, don't quit; simply start again with the current calendar day. Don't worry about catching up.
- Remove distractions like TV, Facebook, work projects, and cell phones.
- Pray and ask for God's help in taking this journey.
- At the end of every reading, there will be scripture and a thought for the day. Use these as a mental and heart focus throughout your day.

John 10:27 says, "My sheep listen to my voice; I know them, and they *follow me*" (emphasis added). Do you hear Him? He's calling us not only to believe in Him but also to follow Him. Are you ready to begin the journey?

CHAPTER 1

FOLLOWING JESUS IN OUR MESSY LIVES

SOMETIMES YOU HAVE TO WALK IT

Sometimes we find ourselves in dark circumstances. It could be the ongoing, crushing stress of a job or maybe a physical struggle that won't go away; possibly it's a marriage that seems hopeless and unfulfilling, an addiction, depression, finances, or a host of other circumstances. What do we do when we have prayed, pleaded, begged, and cried out to God to change the circumstances we find ourselves in and nothing happens? Our situation hasn't improved. Our circumstances haven't gotten better. Now what? We may ask ourselves, "Is God ignoring me? Is God punishing me?" Haven't we all been here at one time or another?

The apostle Paul had some issue, some circumstance, some problem he asked God multiple times to remove. He called it a "thorn in the flesh." (2 Cor. 12:7) No one knows what he was referring to, but we all can relate to begging God to remove something painful from our lives. Instead of removing it, God gave Paul another response. God chose to leave the issue in place and told Paul he needed to depend on God's grace so His power could be seen. Here's what God said to Paul: "Three times I pleaded with the Lord to take it away from me. But he said to me, 'My grace is sufficient for you, for my power is made perfect in weakness.' Therefore I will boast all the more gladly about my weaknesses, so that Christ's power may rest on me" (2 Cor. 12:8–9).

There will be times when we all find ourselves asking God to remove something painful from us. This asking is appropriate, good, and even encouraged in God's word. There will be times, though, when God will tell us no. Not because the situation is punishment. Not because God doesn't care. The reality is that He wants us to depend on His grace so that in our weakness, His power in our lives will be on display. Sometimes we have to walk the path of difficulty to experience this truth. It's in our complete weakness that we discover that Jesus is truly enough.

If you find yourself in some painful, dark circumstances and God doesn't seem to be removing them, maybe it's time for a different prayer like this. "God, if this is a path You want me to walk, then I surrender to You. May Your power work best in my weakness. May You show me that You are all I need. I choose to trust You with my circumstances I don't understand." There is something spiritual, something supernatural, that happens when we humble ourselves like this before God. I can't promise you your circumstances will change, but I *can* promise you that God will change you. When we accept the road God has placed before us, this is where we discover Him being all we need.

Scripture for the Day:

2 Corinthians 12:8–10

Thought for the Day:

In what ongoing circumstance does God want you to trust Him, even if He doesn't remove it? What is keeping you from being willing to walk this path with Jesus?

ISOLATION

One of the worst forms of punishment is solitary confinement. Putting any prisoner in a dark, small, enclosed space for an extended period of time can cause a person to lose his or her mind. There have been numerous documented cases of POWs simply losing the will to live any longer in these conditions. It has been a known fact for millennia that a human being needs interaction with others. To be healthy, we need one another.

Many people live in self-imposed prisons of isolation. Because of some past relational wound, they have concluded that they don't need others and don't need to emotionally bond; therefore, they keep themselves at arm's length relationally. They never let people get past the surface and never expose the depths of their hearts to anyone. They live in emotional isolation, even while they interact daily with others. Their hearts live in the painful state of solitary confinement, while others are completely oblivious to the prison they exist in. They are truly "alone," and they know it.

Did I just describe you? Did I describe someone you know and love? Relational isolation is one of the enemy's greatest tools and biggest lies. Someone may have deeply hurt you. Someone you love may have wounded you to the core of your being. This wound doesn't have to sentence you to a life of isolation. God has something better for you. He made you a relational being. He created you with the need to connect deeply with others. There are over fifty "one another" commands in the Bible. Over fifty times we are told to love one another, comfort one another, pray for one another, encourage one another, bear one another's burdens, and forgive one another—just to name a few. You cannot experience these in all their fullness if you are isolated.

I know you're afraid. I know you don't want to be hurt again. I know you're wondering whether people will accept you. I understand your reluctance to trust one more time. Aren't these fears worth facing rather than the daily pain of your self-imposed isolation? You are missing out on the greatest blessing this earthly experience has to offer outside of Jesus Himself: a relationship with another person. You were made for this. You were designed for this. Now trust Jesus and leave your prison. There is someone out there who needs a person just like you.

Scripture for the Day:

1 Corinthians 12:12–17; Hebrews 10:23–25

Thought for the Day:

How are you protecting yourself from the relationships God wants you to experience? How can you move back into relationships with others? Do you need to go to church, join a life group, be part of a class, or join a team to serve?

THE KEY TO HAPPINESS

"I just want to be happy." Over the years as a pastor, I have heard this phrase countless times. It seems to speak of an inherent desire every person has. We simply want to be happy. The problem isn't in the desire. The dilemma comes in the pursuit. Even though our Constitution says we have the right to pursue happiness, it seems rather elusive to most people. Why are we so unhappy? Why are we so unsatisfied? What is it that grows these feelings of discontent? I believe there is one core issue: selfishness. The reason happiness is elusive to so many is that they pursue it in a way that makes it impossible for them to experience it.

Most in our culture believe happiness is experienced through some type of self-focused pursuit. Therefore, we see individuals pursue money, status, power, pleasure, comfort, convenience, or possessions as a means to discover happiness. They try to do or acquire something to make them happy. It is a self-absorbed existence. The world revolves around them, what they want, how they want it, and what their desires are. Some may wonder, *What's wrong with this?* It's a dead end. This strategy for finding happiness will never make you happy. Selfishness actually perpetuates feelings of unhappiness in us. Numerous studies have shown that overall life satisfaction isn't achieved through a life focused on ourselves. This is the fast track to unhappiness. What studies have shown—and what God's word has said all along—is that true happiness is discovered in serving the needs of others.

That's right! An others-centered life is the quickest way to make yourself happy. You feel down in the dumps? Are you struggling with feelings of dissatisfaction? Do you have general feelings of unhappiness? It's time to get the focus off yourself and on others. The more time you focus on yourself, the more depressed you're going to get. It's time to get up, go make someone else's day, and stop obsessing over yourself; you'll find that making someone else happy will increase your happiness.

Philippians 2:2–5 says, "Then make my joy complete by being like-minded, having the same love, being one in spirit and of one mind. Do nothing out of selfish ambition or vain conceit. Rather, in humility value others above yourselves, not looking to your own interests but each of you to the interests of the others. In your relationships with one another, have the same mindset as Christ Jesus."

There you go. Here are your real keys to happiness. It's time to go serve through a resource center, soup kitchen, after-school program, or mission trip. Sponsor a child or go fix the elderly neighbor's porch. Whatever you do, do something for someone else. "What good will this do?" you may ask. It will make you happy. Try it and see for yourself.

Scripture for the Day:

Philippians 2:1–11

Thought for the Day:

Have you been pursuing happiness or pursuing service to others? If you pursue what Jesus wants, He will throw in happiness as a bonus. Reflect on Matthew 6:33 with this mind-set.

DON'T LET FAILURE DEFINE YOU

It was only a few hours before Peter's epic failure. Jesus had just predicted that someone would betray Him. All the disciples were astonished and horrified at the thought. Peter had just declared his undying loyalty to Jesus, even to the death. At the same time, Judas had already slipped out to secretly meet with the religious leaders to plan Jesus' arrest. It is a story of two failures. It is a story of two men who completely blew it, two individuals who fell so badly and so hard; how could they ever recover from such a personal catastrophe?

Judas betrayed Jesus for thirty pieces of silver and handed Jesus over to the religious leaders to be arrested. Peter, after Jesus was arrested, denied he even knew Jesus—not once but three times. Here in Jesus' greatest hour of need and His darkest moment in life, Peter wasn't there for Him. Peter chose to protect his own skin instead of standing up for Jesus.

This is a story of two men and two catastrophic failures. One man let the failure define and destroy his life; the other found forgiveness and restoration. Judas was so horrified and overcome with remorse that he committed suicide, seeing no way to recover from such a failure. Peter, on the other hand, experienced something different. Peter was able to take his failure to Jesus. His failure didn't define him. His failure didn't determine the rest of his life.

Are you struggling with finding hope in your failure? Maybe it's a failed marriage or marriages; or maybe it's your dark past that haunts you, an abortion, a promiscuous lifestyle, failed finances, or a failed business venture. Maybe a current addiction stalks you like a predator. If you had to give yourself a grade for life, you would give yourself an F. You see your failures as the defining quality of your life. You believe your failures will control and determine your future. Your failures even control what you believe about God. How can God forgive me? How can God accept me? How can God even want me as part of His family? How can I ever be useful to God after all I've done? Maybe God has abandoned me.

Let's return to the story and see an amazing perspective. Jesus knew Peter was about to fail in a way that could destroy him and his future. Peter was one of Jesus' closest friends, but notice how Jesus handled this failure before it even happened. Luke 22:31–32 says, "Simon, Simon, Satan has asked to sift all of you as wheat. But I have prayed for you, Simon, that your faith may not fail. And when you have turned back, strengthen your brothers."

Do you see any condemnation? Do you hear any shock or surprise over Peter's upcoming epic failure? Do you hear even a hint of disappointment? None! What you hear are love, concern, and purpose. "Yes, Peter, you're going to fail hard, but this won't be what defines your life."

Let this give you hope today. Why? Because Peter's failure is worse than anything you've done. He physically lived with Jesus for over three years and saw countless miracles. He witnessed people whom Jesus raised from the dead. He saw multitudes miraculously fed. After all he witnessed, he still denied Him three times. I guarantee you that your failures don't measure up to that! If Jesus could forgive, love, and restore him, then Jesus can do the same for you. If Peter's failure didn't define him and his future, then your failures don't have to define your life any longer. It's time to get out from the shadows of your past and step into the light of the life Jesus has for you. Jesus' forgiveness defines us. His love assures us of a future.

The road Judas took was hopeless. Believing you're beyond the reaches of God's grace and forgiveness is a self-destructive path. This is the lie the enemy wants you to believe. Hear the voice of your Good Shepherd today. He's calling you to come to Him. It is your relationship with Him, not your failure, that defines you. Take all your failures to Jesus; embrace His forgiveness and bask in His acceptance of you. Don't believe the lies any longer. Don't allow the lies to define your future. Give all the broken pieces of your life to Jesus and watch Him give you a future and a hope. Watch in awe as He redefines who you are.

Scripture for the Day:

Romans 8:1, 31–39

Thought for the Day:

Have you been allowing your failures to define your future rather than the forgiveness and restoration found only in Jesus? Jesus is ready to give you your future back. Are you willing to receive it from Him?

HARD SEASONS

Sometimes life just gets hard. I'm not talking about having a bad day or a momentary painful circumstance. I'm talking about when we enter into something longer, more profound, darker, and ongoing. There are periods of our lives when we simply enter hard seasons. For whatever reason, the joy is difficult to find; you feel trapped by your life. You feel as though you are suffocating emotionally. Your thoughts tend to be negative and hopeless. Relationally you feel isolated as if no one really understands you. Sure, there are people around you, but you still feel alone. During these times we can even feel isolated from God. Where is God when I need Him the most? Where is His help when my soul feels crushed? Deep down you know there is no shortcut out of this. There is no quick fix. You can't just microwave a solution to make it all better. No, you're in a hard season. How do I know all this? I've been in hard seasons too.

Maybe this describes the season you're in right now. What do we do when we find ourselves in hard seasons? How do we navigate our lives through these tough times? Is there any hope? Of course there is, but the process isn't easy. Remember, it's a hard season. The first step is to stop looking for the easy way out. This sets you up for only more disappointment. You just have to let that one go.

One of the most profound, life-altering truths I have experienced over the years is simply this: refuse to quit. I know—you were looking for something more spiritual. Perseverance is a biblical truth. Perseverance is what we need to get through the hard seasons of life. Perseverance is one of the most spiritual and essential qualities we need in this hard life. Hebrews 10:35–36 says, "So do not throw away your confidence; it will be richly rewarded. You need to persevere so that when you have done the will of God, you will receive what he has promised."

What does this look like? It is choosing to trust God, even when you can't see Him. It is choosing to follow Him in obedience, even though you don't feel like it. It is treating people with love, even though you feel you have none to give. It is trusting in His forgiveness when you fail. It is believing in His love for you when you wonder why He does. It is getting out of bed one more day and choosing to do the right thing, even though you don't know how. It is believing God is right there with you, even though you can't sense His presence. It is praying and begging God for the strength for one more day, even though you feel your prayers don't go past the ceiling. It is refusing to listen to the lies in your mind that tell you to throw away your trust in God. It is also remembering and trusting that there is a reward for this type of perseverance. When you don't think it matters, perseverance reminds you that it does.

If you find yourself in a hard season, please don't quit. I know you're hurting. I know it's confusing. I understand that it's painful. Please don't quit. Don't quit on yourself and don't quit on God. Remember, this is a season, and seasons change. This one won't last forever. You will come out the other side. God won't allow this hard season to define your life or your future. You will experience all God has promised. I know this because of the hard seasons I have experienced; they have made the promises of God that much sweeter. They have made my relationship with God that much closer. The same will be true for you. May God give you the grace for one more day. Don't quit.

Scripture for the Day:

2 Corinthians 1:8–11

Thought for the Day:

Consider making a simple commitment to God each day, praying, "Lord, I choose to trust You today. Please give me the perseverance for one more day."

DO YOU HAVE MARGINS?

As I write this on my computer, automatic margins are created. There are margins on all sides of the page. Those who are reading this page are glad for the margins. Why? Because without margins, the text would be much more difficult to read. The margins make not only the writing more enjoyable but also the reading. Margins make this whole experience better.

Margins are important not only for reading and writing but also for life. Margins make our entire life experience better. We all have a tendency to reduce the margins in our lives. I struggle with this issue. I want to see how productive I can be. I want to get done as much as possible. "Get up early and work late" has always been my motto. I push the lines of my life right out to the edge of the page. I'm going to put as much on the life page as possible. We erroneously think this is the best way to live, but then we wonder why we are always tired and feel stressed— why we can't relax, have trouble sleeping, feel joyless, and maybe even find ourselves irritable at those around us. No margins!

If there was anyone who felt the demands on His time, it was Jesus. Can you imagine what it would have been like to have multitudes always flocking to see you because you could heal them, feed them, and give them hope? Yet even in His chaotic travels from town to town, Jesus built margins in His life. One of the many times we see Jesus doing this is right after He miraculously fed five thousand men plus women and children; therefore, it is safe to be thinking of a group in the twelve- to fifteen-thousand-person range. The people were so in awe of this event that they were immediately ready to make Jesus their king. John 6:15 says, "Jesus, knowing that they intended to come and make him king by force, withdrew again to a mountain by himself."

Now if this were us, after a three-day stint of teaching, healing, and now supernaturally feeding this mass crowd, we would burn the midnight oil. We would establish a follow-up strategy and begin identifying the key leaders within the crowd. Well, now, this went so well; we'd probably begin the formation of a promotional video for the next town we'd go to. Notice what Jesus did as He rode this big wave of momentum? He left. He walked away. He headed for the hills to be alone and maintain His margins. He knew that without margins, He would lose priority, focus, and mission. It was in those margins where He could connect deeply with the heart of His Father, who would empower Him in the chaos of ministry.

If Jesus knew He needed margins, who are we to think we can follow Jesus effectively without them? How often do we say or think, "I don't have time to read my Bible" or, "I don't have time to pray"? Or even, "I don't have time to worship"? The reason we don't have time is that we are unwilling to "slip away" as Jesus did. We're unwilling to create margins. We're unwilling to slow down, relax, and walk away for a while. If Jesus walked away from twelve thousand to fifteen thousand people, who were all chanting His name, who are we to think we can't slip away from whatever is so important to us?

I know we all need to experience Jesus in the frenzied pace of life. But don't you ever get tired of treating Jesus as if you're going through a drive-through at a fast-food place? Jesus is waiting for you in the margins. Why not create some margins and go experience Jesus there? It is in the space we create where we are empowered for the journey. He's waiting. Isn't it time to "slip away"?

Scripture for the Day:

Mark 1:35–39

Thought for the Day:

Do you need to create some margins in your life? Where can you slip away from the chaos, even if for only a few moments? Where can you create some extended margins with more time? Do you need to stop telling yourself this is impossible? Pray, asking God for the help to create margins.

SPIRITUAL GROWTH IS MESSY

I absolutely love watching my grandchildren grow. It is fascinating to me how quickly they begin to learn, adapt, and mature in their knowledge and abilities. My granddaughter is just on the verge of crawling. She gets on all fours, she starts rocking back and forth, and sometimes she even picks her knees up and balances herself on her toes and hands alone. It's as if she knows something more is supposed to happen here; she just doesn't have it figured out yet. She then tries to move an arm or knee and takes a face-plant into the carpet. We all cheer and shout, "Good job!" Yeah, but she failed to crawl. Why are we cheering? We cheer because she's trying. We cheer because she's trying to grow. We cheer because we don't want her to be discouraged. We know growth is messy.

I believe this is a great example of our own spiritual journey. Once we experience a spiritual birth by accepting Jesus, we should move on and grow to maturity in Christ. But this journey is a messy one. It's certainly not a straight, upward line. It's a pretty crooked line filled with ups and downs, mountaintops, and lots of failures. You see, this is what makes spiritual growth so messy; we fail often. Just when we're trying to take some new step of obedience, we take another face-plant right into the ground. Often we're left wondering what is wrong with us. *Why can't I walk, run, and endure spiritually?* Answer: spiritual growth is messy.

We must come to understand that failure is how we all learn. It is how our children and grandchildren learn, and it is how we learn to follow Jesus in this life. I see so many believers in Jesus beat themselves up daily because of their struggle. The struggle with sin is part of the journey. Look at what the apostle Paul said in Romans 7:14–15. "We know that the law is spiritual; but I am unspiritual, sold as a slave to sin. I do not understand what I do. For what I want to do I do not do, but what I hate I do."

That pretty much sums up this life, don't you think? The problem isn't with the word of God; the problem is that I can't seem to follow it all the time. I fall. I fail. I know I'm supposed to be something more than I am, yet I still blow it. I still do things I hate. What's my problem? Nothing. Learning to follow Jesus and grow to maturity is a very messy process. We fail a lot in this process. Failure is how we learn.

Now, I'm not trying to make any excuses for our behavior and sin. What I want you to see is that God knows you're going to blow it. He knows the journey to maturity is lined with failures. He knows failure is how we learn. This is why He has His amazing forgiveness built in to this equation. He has enough forgiveness for the messiness of your growth. What He wants from you is another try, not perfection.

If you have been beating yourself up because you just took yet another face-plant, please don't quit. Your failures don't define you or your future. They are the stepping-stones that will propel you to maturity. God is cheering you on, not condemning you. He's calling you to try to follow Him once again. He rejoices over each new step of growth in your life, no matter how small. He knows spiritual growth is messy. Get back up on those wobbly legs, grab the hand of Jesus as firmly as you know how, and take that step. Whether you get one step or ten, you're going to fall again. Jesus will be right there to rejoice in your progress, not criticizing you for falling. The messiness of your journey doesn't hinder Jesus from rejoicing over your life any more than the messiness of my granddaughter's journey of learning to crawl hinders me from rejoicing over her. She is my delight. You are God's delight as well. Growth is just messy.

Scripture for the Day:

Romans 8:31–39

Thought for the Day:

Have you been allowing the discouragement that comes from failure to cause you not to try again? Is it time to get back up? Is it time to stop allowing the messiness of your journey to define your journey?

THE MYTH OF THE EASY LIFE

Now that I'm fifty years old, have thirty years of ministry experience, have been married for over twenty-eight years, and have two married daughters and two grandkids, I have abandoned a once-held myth. What is it? "Life gets easier with age." It's simply not true. Of course, certain things got easier. We're not raising kids anymore. We're more financially secure than when we were younger. I'm no longer starting a church in a grade school with no money and only thirty people. But to think that life overall is easier really isn't true. Some battles are over, but others took their place. The belief that life is supposed to get easy as we age will only make us miserable if we hold onto it. This myth can set us up for great disappointment and even keep us from following Jesus as we get older. Why do I say this?

The Bible is very clear that we live in a broken world that sin has corrupted. We live among people who are broken and corrupted by sin. We as individuals are broken and corrupted by sin. Put those three ingredients into our lives, and the easy life becomes a myth. This is why Jesus said in John 16:33, "I have told you these things, so that in me you may have peace. In this world you will have trouble. But take heart! I have overcome the world." That's certainly not one of Jesus' most popular promises, but nonetheless, it's still a promise. In this world we will (not *may*) have trouble. This world is going to be hard.

Now, I don't mean to discourage anyone. That is certainly not my point in writing this. I just think we should all live in the same reality Jesus describes. To have the expectation that life will be hard isn't a defeatist mentality but rather mental and spiritual preparation. I talk to so many believers who think and act as if something were wrong when life gets hard. Why is this happening? Why did God do this? Why did God allow this? Where is God in this? I have seen hard times destroy people emotionally and spiritually. There is such a fast-held belief that life should be easy and get easier that people are completely ill equipped for the very thing Jesus promised ... trouble.

Notice that Jesus said, "I have told you these things, so that in me you may have peace." When we expect life to be hard, we are much more apt to experience Jesus being our peace in the midst of it. The answer for when things get tough is Jesus, not a change in circumstances. If we never expect life to be hard, we'll never expect Jesus to be the answer. We'll never go to Him and allow Him to be enough for us. We'll never learn to rely on Him, drawing from the life He can pour into us. We'll never experience His presence at our point of need and His power to face the challenges. Sometimes I cause the trouble I face in this world. I create it.

After all these years, I still struggle with sin. It shows up in my attitudes, in my actions toward my wife, and even in my pride. Sometimes others cause it. Their sinful actions toward me impact my life in negative ways. At other times, this fallen world causes the trouble. The trouble can be in the form of our broken government, broken culture, and even the broken environment when we face natural disasters. The answer is still that Jesus is enough. Can I experience His peace, no matter what form of trouble I face?

So if you're waiting and wondering when life is going to get easier, the answer is that I have no idea. It might do so for a season. I hope it does for you. I do believe there are times when God gives us seasons of blessings. These seasons, though, don't change the promise Jesus gave. There will still be trouble in this world, *but* don't live in fear of it. Jesus has overcome this world, and His peace can be our reality. The trouble of this world doesn't have to define our lives as followers of Jesus. Jesus wants to define our lives if we will let Him, no matter what.

Scripture for the Day:

2 Corinthians 1:8–11

Thought for the Day:

Are you spending all your time wondering when things are going to get better? Or are you going to Jesus and letting Him make *you* better?

DEALING WITH TEMPTATION

As I sit here in my living room, writing this, our cat sits outside on our porch with her eyes fixed on the bird feeder. It's really a pathetic sight. She watches a flurry of bird activity as the birds feast on the morsels my wife and I put out for them. She sits maybe twenty feet away. You see the longing in her eyes, the desire to pounce, to hunt, to be a successful bird killer, but it will never happen. She's too fat, slow, and old. Those birds are living in complete safety. It's as if they mock her with each flight into the feeder. She just sits and longs for something that will never happen. Truthfully, it looks like torture. I think she would be much happier if she simply walked away. Ended the torment. Had some catnip or something!

As I watch our cat, I can't help but think about our own struggles with temptations in this life. It's not that we can eliminate them altogether. That's impossible. Let's face it; temptation has a way of finding us. There are plenty of times, though, when we do have a choice. Often we're just like the cat. We torment ourselves by willfully putting ourselves in front of temptation. With each exposure the temptation grows stronger, the urges more intense; the desires increase, and before you know it, the temptation wins again. The Bible talks about temptation. First Corinthians 10:13 says, "No temptation has overtaken you except what is common to mankind. And God is faithful; he will not let you be tempted beyond what you can bear. But when you are tempted, he will also provide a way out so that you can endure it."

I've talked to a lot of people over the years who told me they just couldn't help themselves. The temptation was just too intense. God allowed them to be tempted beyond what they could endure. Are you sure? Maybe the problem was simple overexposure. Often the way out of temptation, which God provides, is to remove ourselves from it. Sometimes this answer is so obvious that we miss it. Instead, we continually expose ourselves to the very thing we should be running away from. Then we fail and wonder why God didn't help us.

What temptation are you facing, when the help God gives you is to remove yourself from it? You can turn the TV off. You can choose to use your computer at home only when your spouse is around. You don't have to go out to lunch with the handsome (or gorgeous) coworker. You don't need to engage in the secret online chat. You don't have to keep looking at houses that are way out of your budget. You don't have to drive by that particular liquor store. You have a choice. Some temptations we must simply choose to avoid. If we don't, like my cat, we only torment ourselves. The difference is that our cat has no way of catching those birds. You, on the other hand, have ample ways of allowing temptation to catch you. Make the hard choice today. Walk away! You'll be so glad you did.

Scripture for the Day:

James 1:12–15

Thought for the Day:

What excuses are you making for not walking away? Is there a close friend to whom you can share your temptation for some accountability?

THE IMPORTANCE OF REST

Rest has never been a strong suit of mine. I'm an activity guy, the proverbial "pedal to the metal" kind of person. I just have that "need for speed" in my daily schedule. I like the fast-paced environment, where I have the challenge to see just how much I can accomplish in one day. Rest ... who needs it? I'll rest someday when I'm old. (Oh wait, I'm already fifty!) That's not old, by the way. Although all these phrases accurately describe my personality (besides the old part), I'm learning the significance of rest. Let me share with you what this adrenaline junky is learning.

First, I want to be like Jesus. Since Jesus modeled rest, it would be a good idea for me to do so as well. If Jesus in His humanity needed rest, why do I think I don't need it?

> But Jesus often withdrew to lonely places and prayed.
> (Luke 5:16)

> When Jesus heard what had happened, he withdrew by
> boat privately to a solitary place. (Matt. 14:13)

There were plenty of times when Jesus simply withdrew from the demands of ministry, the expectations of people, and the public spotlight. There were times when He wasn't teaching, wasn't healing, and wasn't engaged in the constant verbal barrage of the religious leaders. He simply withdrew from it all. He went off the grid. This is something I need to do periodically as well.

Second, I would like to be the pastor of Foothills for at least another twenty years. I want to have the energy, passion, and drive to make a significant difference for the kingdom of God for at least another two decades. I don't want to burn out somewhere along the process. I want to continually give you the very best I have every week. My love for

Jesus and for those I serve compels me to give my very best. Therefore, I need to protect this. Fatigue and weariness rob not only me but you as well. Rest is what protects my best for Jesus and for you.

As I have tried to apply this rest principle in my life, I have had times of great success and complete failure. I'm still learning. I don't have it all figured out yet. Here's what I have discovered so far.

Rest dramatically improves my relationship with God. There are times when I need to be away from ministry for more than a day or weekend. I need some significant rest. The hectic activity of ministry can actually become a hindrance to spiritual intimacy. I don't just need Jesus to help me do ministry; I need Jesus for me. I need to connect deeply with Him for my sake, for my growth, for my needs, and in my pain. How can I authentically communicate with all of you how to connect deeply with Him if it isn't real and genuine in my own life? When I choose to rest, Jesus' voice gets louder, clearer, and more distinct. The competing noise is so much less that this weary sheep can identify the voice of his Shepherd leading him to those quiet waters to drink. My experience with Jesus helps me to genuinely communicate with you.

Rest dramatically improves my relationships with others. Our hectic pace negatively impacts our relationship not only with God but also with others. Let me illustrate. When my wife, Lisa, and I travel in Mexico for vacation, I like to drive. I enjoy the traffic laws in Mexico. Most of them are suggestions. Perfect! This can create some very interesting driving moments. Lisa and I can be talking in the car nonstop, but when the speed increases and the traffic multiplies, the concentration required to drive multiplies. When this happens, the conversation gets less and less. Pretty soon Lisa gets a simple yes and no. It's not a time for deep communication. It's time to keep,my eye on the two cars driving at us in our lane!

When our pace increases, communication decreases. Yet when we slow the speed by which we travel and remove complications from journey, the communication and relationships can flourish.

If you've been struggling to connect with God and others, the simple solution may be rest. Sometimes taking a rest is the most spiritual and profound thing you can do. We don't value rest in our culture. Yet if we read the word of God, we will see that the principle of rest begins at creation and runs through the entire Bible. God commanded it, Jesus practiced it, and often we ignore it. God is waiting to talk to you, and I'm sure there is someone very close to you who would love your full attention as well. Who knew we could love God and others better because of one simple solution ... rest?

Scripture for the Day:

Exodus 20 (notice the seventh-day rest)

Thought for the Day:

Does rest need to be more of a priority in your life so you can love God and others better? Do you see the connection between rest and relationships?

LIFE: THE SUM OF OUR CHOICES

We live in a day and age when embracing the mind-set of a victim is the norm. No one is individually responsible anymore. "My circumstances must be someone else's fault. I flunked my class because I had a bad teacher. I got fired from my job because I had a mean boss. I got a speeding ticket because I drive a red Camaro (police target red cars, you know). I have no money because I keep having bad luck. I spilled hot coffee on myself, so I sued the company that made it. I got a divorce because my spouse was a jerk. My wife drove me to drink. My husband caused me to have an affair. My spouse is the reason I'm so unhappy." The list could go on and on. Even criminals don't need to be responsible for their behavior. God forbid they should accidentally injure themselves while they rob your house. They might sue you ... and win! Now they are the victims.

If you read the word of God at all, you will quickly see that God doesn't allow us to play the victim card in this life. Of course bad things happen to us. People wound us, circumstances blindside us, and tragedies scar us. But regardless of what horrible experiences we are dealt with in this life, God gives us the tremendous power of choice. Regardless of the events, circumstances, and people in our lives, we are the sum of our choices. We don't have to allow the wind of circumstances to define our lives. God has given us our wills as a rudder to make choices that will set the course of our lives. You have the power of choice. Use it!

Deuteronomy 30:19–20 says, "This day I call the heavens and the earth as witnesses against you that I have set before you life and death, blessings and curses. Now *choose* life, so that you and your children may live and that you may love the Lord your God, listen to his voice, and hold fast to him. For the Lord is your life, and he will give you many years in the land he swore to give to your fathers, Abraham, Isaac and Jacob" (emphasis added).

It is the choices you make that will be the key to your life. It won't be people, events, or circumstances. It won't be good luck or bad luck. It will be you. You have the power to make choices that will breathe either life into your circumstances or death. It will be your choices that will bring either blessings or curses. God has given you this choice. I know this isn't a very popular message in our day, but it needs to be said. If you don't like the life you are currently living, make different choices. You are the one responsible for your life, not anyone else. Galatians 6:7–8 says, "Do not be deceived: God cannot be mocked. A man reaps what he sows. Whoever sows to please their flesh, from the flesh will reap destruction; whoever sows to please the Spirit, from the Spirit will reap eternal life."

God has set up this world to operate on this principle: you will harvest what you plant. What you put into the soil of your life you will harvest as experiences. If you plant bitterness, you will experience bitterness in your life. If you plant dishonesty, you will experience dishonesty. If you withhold love, then don't be surprised when love is withheld from you. If you plant a critical spirit, then expect to be criticized. If you plant mistrust and insecurity, then get ready to be lonely.

Now, of course, we will all experience a degree of these negative things just by living in this fallen world. The difference is that these experiences won't define us. They don't have the power of death and decay on our lives. Instead, we choose to follow Jesus. We choose the Spirit. We choose to love God and others. We choose to be obedient to the word of God regardless. We choose life. What life are you choosing? Our lives aren't the sum of our circumstances. Our lives are the sum of our choices.

Maybe you have spent a lot of time blaming others for where you are today. *Surely my situation is someone else's fault.* How about you choose life today. Regardless of the circumstances, maybe many you had nothing to do with, you are still making choices. It isn't the events in this life that define us. It is the choices we make in response to them. God gave you the power to plant life or death, blessings or curses. Don't you think it's time to choose a different life? He's calling you to more. Choose life today!

Scripture for the Day:

Deuteronomy 30:11–20

Thought for the Day:

How are your choices defining your life? Where do you need to take responsibility for the harvest of your life and make different choices?

ARE YOU DRIFTING?

If you fly much, you know it's pretty crucial for the plane to stay on course and reach its intended destination. Nobody wants to board a plane in JFK, heading to LAX, and end up in Portland, Oregon. Even one degree off the intended flight pattern can be a pretty big deal. It's easy to think that one degree off doesn't matter much. But consider this: for every one degree off course a plane flies, it will be off target one mile for every sixty miles flown. If you decided to fly around the equator, flying only one degree off would put you five hundred miles off your intended target. You see, the longer you fly off course, the greater the distance you travel from your original destination. Drifting off course even a little can take you to places you never intended to go. Hebrews 2:1 says, "We must pay the most careful attention, therefore, to what we have heard, so that we do not drift away."

What a great word for us today. As followers of Jesus, it is so easy to drift. Drifting spiritually is hard to recognize. It's difficult to detect. Drifting is subtle, quiet, and slow. It simply doesn't set off any internal alarms in us. In fact, we aren't even aware of it until we've traveled long enough to wonder, *How did I end up here?* You were drifting. Maybe you were only one or two degrees off course, but you traveled for years like that. Possibly you observed others on their journey and saw they were many degrees off course. It was obvious they were flying in the wrong direction. You were thankful that wasn't you. Yet you were still a little off course. You consoled yourself: "At least I'm headed in the right direction." Yet the drifting in your life continued. A little compromise here, a little character flaw there, and a little secret fleshly indulgence no one knew about. Maybe in and of themselves, these actions weren't game changers, but the drifting continued. Now, after many years, you are finally waking up to the gravity of the situation. You are way off course. *How did I end up here?* You were drifting.

How does one guard himself or herself from this spiritual drift? Go back to Hebrews 2; the author tells us to "pay the most careful attention." Just as a pilot must pay careful attention to the instruments of the plane, we must pay careful attention to our lives as well. We can't afford to allow ourselves to go to "sleep at the wheel," as it is said. So what am I supposed to pay careful attention to? First, we must pay careful attention to the flight plan for our lives, which is recorded in the word of God. If we don't read, know, and follow the word of God, our lives have no other option than to be off course. We simply can't fly our lives by your feelings. We need the objective standard of the word of God.

Second, we must evaluate our journey based on the word of God. Are we following the coordinates given? Are we following what they say about our relationships, marriages, mission, values, money, and purpose? God's word gives us clear directions in these and other areas. Do we submit our journey to the coordinates of God's word? If we aren't paying attention to these navigational truths, our lives will be radically off course. For some it may take a while, even years, but the result of drifting is the same for all.

Sometimes we all need a wake-up call. Maybe now is the time for you. As you have been reading this, you know you've been drifting. Maybe you have been spiritually and morally drifting for years, and the reality of this decision is starting to sink in. It's never too late for a course correction. It's never too late to begin to "pay attention." Today is always the right day to go back to Jesus and submit every area of your life to Him and His word. You don't have to drift. The destination your drifting is taking you toward can be refused. Ephesians 5:14 says, "This is why it is said: 'Wake up, sleeper, rise from the dead, and Christ will shine on you.'" Jesus is ready to help you. He's ready to shine on you and give you direction. Sometimes it's as simple as waking up. The drifting can stop today.

Scripture for the Day:

Hebrews 3:12–15

Thought for the Day:

Okay, let's be honest with ourselves. Have you been drifting? Have you been drifting morally, spiritually, relationally? Or in your integrity, behavior, and attitudes? Have you been paying attention to yourself and to your relationship with Jesus? Are you off course? How far? Are you willing to make some navigational adjustments?

RESPONDING TO OVERWHELMING EVIL

This week there was another senseless shooting. This time it was in my home state, about one hundred miles from where I live. Ten lives have been lost while thousands have been impacted in some way forever. Evil showed its face once again with devastating consequences. We are all brokenhearted over the loss and impacted deeply by the magnitude of such violence and hatred for human life. What are we to do? How are we to respond? Sometimes the overwhelming evil in this world can create a hopelessness to stand against it in our very souls. Even when I look beyond my own state, I see that this world is filled with such violence, death, and brokenness of humanity that they stagger the heart and mind.

There is a scene from *The Two Towers*, the second movie in *The Lord of the Rings*, that captures how I feel at times. It is at the darkest and most hopeless point of the movie. The enemy has broken through all the defenses. The darkness is just about to overwhelm humanity. The king and his army have retreated as far back as they possibly can. King Théoden says, "What can men do against such reckless hate?" Good question! Sometimes don't you feel the same way? This world just seems to be filled with such reckless hatred that any response to it almost seems pointless. Well, if you remember, in the movie Aragorn says, "Ride out with me. Ride out to meet them." Let reckless evil meet reckless goodness. If you don't remember what happens next, I suggest you go watch the movie.

Romans 12:21 says, "Do not be overcome by evil, but overcome evil with good." The reckless evil of this fallen world must meet the reckless goodness of God's people. Horrific events remind us that there are two distinct kingdoms: God's kingdom and Satan's kingdom. We are in the middle of a spiritual battle. No government or political process will fix it. It is a spiritual battle between the forces of darkness and the forces of light. Evil will be overcome only with good. Reckless evil must come face-to-face with the reckless goodness of God's people. Good is stronger than evil. Light will dispel darkness. God wins, and Satan loses.

With this being true, instead of allowing your heart to wither in despair, choose to do something good in response to evil. This is what following Jesus looks like. Believers should "ride out to meet it." I'm not talking about physically confronting evil but spiritually confronting it. How? Will you recklessly pray against it? Will you practically love others in response to it? Will you passionately meet needs where you see them? Will you profoundly shine the light of Jesus where you see the darkness of hopelessness? Will you thoroughly get involved in the kingdom conflict instead of simply being an observer? Will you joyfully serve? Will you fearlessly pursue God's agenda for your life rather than your own? Half-hearted attempts at goodness won't battle reckless evil. If we want to see a change from the reckless hatred, then we need a reckless love. Evil is recklessly abandoned to its agenda to destroy. Are we recklessly abandoned to follow Jesus?

May we not allow our hearts to be overcome and overwhelmed by all the evil we see. May we recklessly follow Jesus in this life as we overcome evil with His goodness.

Scripture for the Day:

1 Peter 5:7–9

Thought for the Day:

Doing nothing in response to evil puts us on a fast track to being overwhelmed by it. How can you actively respond to evil you see with acts of goodness? Now trust Jesus and go do something good.

DEALING WITH STRESS

Stress is simply a reality of this life. Sometimes it is fast, intense, and short lived. At other times it is the grueling weight of an ongoing journey with no end in sight. Then there are those seasons of our lives when it feels like both have become our reality simultaneously. One thing is for certain: stress can be a serious thing.

A number of years ago, I almost allowed stress to destroy my life. We were in the middle of a building project at the church. We were expanding and remodeling our auditorium, expanding our children's ministry space, and remodeling a five-thousand-square-foot office building for our growing staff needs. Did I mention we were doing all this at the same time? There is one more dynamic I need to mention; one of our staff members died of cancer during this period. She was a very dear and close personal friend. The pressures of being at the helm of a growing church, overseeing a building project, and experiencing personal grief took me to a place I don't ever want to go to again.

I praise God I had people in my life during that time who allowed me to get healthy again. They loved me enough to help me recover from the burnout I was experiencing. What did I do? The process is much too complex for this type of book, but I can share with you some foundational steps I believe will help you navigate the stress you might be experiencing right now.

Deal with your stress by trusting Jesus. I don't want this to sound cliché, but we have to learn to take our stress and overloaded lives to Jesus and find rest in Him. Isn't this what Jesus promised? Matthew 11:28 says, "Come to me, all you who are weary and burdened, and I will give you rest."

If this is the promise, where is the rest? We have the weary and burdened thing figured out. I believe there is a misunderstanding with experiencing this promise. What is it? This next verse sheds some light on it. Romans 15:13 says, "May the God of hope fill you with all joy and peace as you trust in him, so that you may overflow with hope by the power of the Holy Spirit."

Notice that joy and peace are the results of "as you trust in Him." Joy and peace are the results of trust, not merely belief. It has been my experience that many people believe, but few people trust. It's only in the trusting that we find rest. It's only in the trusting that we experience Jesus and His resources. It's only in the trusting that we genuinely take our brokenness to the feet of Jesus. It's only in the trusting that I finally give up and allow God to have full access to my life. Sometimes it is the pain and agony of stress that make us so desperate that Jesus now becomes the only option we have left. Are you dealing with stress, believing in Jesus, or trusting in Jesus? There is a tremendous difference.

Deal with your stress by trusting others. Hebrews 10:24–25 says, "And let us consider how we may spur one another on toward love and good deeds, not giving up meeting together, as some are in the habit of doing, but encouraging one another."

God didn't intend for you to go through the rigors of this world alone. I realize our culture glorifies the "lone ranger" mentality, but this is a myth. The more you isolate yourself, the more stress will multiply in your life. Solitary confinement is one of the harshest punishments a human can experience, yet countless people sentence themselves to this horror every day by refusing to trust and allow others into their lives. This results in self-inflicted stress. God never intended you to experience this prison. There are over fifty "one another" commands in the New Testament. Repeatedly, we are told to love one another, pray for one another, encourage one another, and forgive one another, just to name a few. When we don't experience the relational priorities of God's word, our stress levels will go up. To successfully deal with stress is to grow in our trust and commitment to the Bible's definition of relationships. I know this requires a risk on your part, but it is a risk worth taking. I know some people have let you down, disappointed you, and even wounded you. I realize this may sound crazy, but try again. Trust Jesus to bring people into your life worth trusting. This is His design for your life and your stress.

Stress is never going away in this life. If our desire is never to be stressed, then we're not living in reality. We live in a broken world among broken people. Stress is here to stay. We can learn to trust Jesus more and trust others to come alongside as we journey through this brokenness. May God give you the courage to trust more and stress less in the days ahead.

Scripture for the Day:

Philippians 4:4–9

Thought for the Day:

Think about the difference between belief and trust. Belief can often simply be a mental exercise, whereas trust requires action or risk of some type. How much do you truly trust Jesus with your life and stress? How much do you trust others? Do you have a small number of trusted friends?

CHAPTER 2

CHANGED BY HIS LOVE

GOD WILL NEVER STOP LOVING YOU

Love can make people do a lot of crazy things. Throughout history, there are plenty of well-known, crazy love stories. Maybe you're familiar with some of them. Of course there's Romeo and Juliet, Cleopatra and Mark Antony, Lancelot and Guinevere. Even the Taj Mahal, which is one of the most recognizable structures in the world, was built by Emperor Shah Jahan in memory of his wife, who died giving birth. The building is a symbol of his eternal love for her. It seems that some of the most famous love stories in history end rather badly. How about one with a good ending? There is one! It's God's ongoing love story for you. Do you know there is nothing you can do that would make God stop loving you? Read how God's love for you is described. Romans 8:38–39 says, "For I am convinced that neither death nor life, neither angels nor demons, neither the present nor the future, nor any powers, neither height nor depth, nor anything else in all creation, will be able to separate us from the love of God that is in Christ Jesus our Lord."

How does God feel about you today? How would you answer this question? Maybe you're thinking that it depends on how "good" you were today. Do you think God is angry with you? Maybe you feel He is disinterested or rather indifferent toward you. Quite possibly you're convinced that God doesn't really want to hear from you today. Some people also feel that God is very judgmental toward them. How about you?

The truth is that God loves you today as much as He ever has. In fact, there is nothing you can do to stop Him from loving you. There is nothing that can separate you from God's love for you. Your current behavior, past behavior, bad attitude, broken relationships, epic failure last week, addiction (which haunts your life), ongoing insecurities, painful circumstances, or even hell itself cannot stop God from being passionately in love with you!

God's love for you isn't based on your performance, behavior, success, or accomplishments. It's not based on your obedience, religious activities, or the lack thereof. God's love for you is completely unconditional. It is founded completely on Him and has nothing to do with you at all. If you think God doesn't love you because of your life, your past, or your mistakes, nothing could be further from the truth.

Over the years I have had countless conversations with people about going to church. Often they respond by saying something about how God wouldn't like it and the walls would cave in if they attended, or a lightning bolt would zap them. You get the picture. They simply believe they've done too much and gone too far. Maybe this is how you feel today. God's love for you is as constant and extreme today as the first day you were born. Nothing has stopped God's love for you, and He will never stop loving you.

Scripture for the Day:

Ephesians 3:16–19

Thought for the Day:

Have you been trying to earn God's love? Have you decided you're beyond hope of receiving God's love? How about periodically spending the day by thanking God for how profoundly He already loves you?

GOD'S LOVE DOESN'T DIMINISH

When my two girls were young, we used to play a game about how much we loved one another. My daughter would say, "Daddy, I love you this much." Of course, as she said this, she stretched out her little arms as far as they would go.

I would say, "I love you this much," as I stretched out my arms as far as they would go. As my girls got older, our game included more descriptions such as, "I love you a million red M&Ms" or "I love you a million chocolate kisses." When the *Toy Story* movie came out, we borrowed from Buzz Lightyear and just said, "To infinity and beyond." In other words, our love could never be diminished.

This is how God's love for us is described in His word. Not only is God's love for us constant; we can never diminish it either. Read these descriptions of God's love for us:

> And I pray that you, being rooted and established in love, may have power, together with all the Lord's holy people, to grasp how wide and long and high and deep is the love of Christ, and to know this love that surpasses knowledge—that you may be filled to the measure of all the fullness of God. (Eph. 3:17–19)

> The Lord appeared to us in the past, saying, "I have loved you with an everlasting love; I have drawn you with unfailing kindness." (Jer. 31:3)

God's love for you is enormously big! If you asked God how much He loves you, it would be beyond what you could fully understand. God's love for you is infinite. It's everlasting. It's eternal. It's as big as He is. It is beyond your full human comprehension. The amazing thing about the size of God's love for you is that you can never diminish it. There is nothing you can do to limit the vastness of God's love for you. God has an unending, unstoppable, eternal supply of it for each one of us, and this includes you.

Some people feel as if they can get to the end of God's love for them … God's love runs out. God has had enough. It's this wrong belief that our bad behavior can use up all of God's love or maybe some of it. Not so! Maybe you feel as if you've run out of chances with God, that somehow your mistakes have diminished His love for you in some way. God loves you less today because of some mistakes or behaviors you regret. Here is the truth from His own word: God's love for you has not diminished one bit since the moment you took your first breath. Nothing you have ever done or will ever do will diminish God's everlasting love for you.

Scripture for the Day:

Psalm 103:11

Thought for the Day:

Do you think God loves other people more than He loves you? Do you feel as if there are behaviors from your past or inconsistencies of your present that limit how much of God's love you can experience? Part of learning how to follow Jesus is embracing just how much He profoundly loves you. Today would be a great day to start.

GOD WILL NEVER STOP
REACHING OUT TO YOU

If you work for a telemarketing company, please forgive me for what I'm about to say. The truth is, I absolutely hate getting phone calls from solicitors. Often these people are relentless. I remember once getting the same phone call from the same company at the same time every day for weeks. I knew who it was because of the caller ID. The situation was a battle of the wills. I was going to refuse to answer until the people at this company quit calling. The problem was … they didn't. Finally, in one moment of frustration and desperation, I grabbed the phone and screamed, "Quit calling me!" and hung up immediately. The phone calls actually stopped after that, but I also felt guilty for being so rude. I'm sure I could have gotten the same response by being polite. Note to self: next time.

Telemarketers are actually a good example of how God's love compels Him to continue reaching out to us. In fact, God is much more relentless in His pursuit of us than any telemarketer. They may eventually stop, but God never will.

> For God so loved the world that he gave his one and only Son, that whoever believes in him shall not perish but have eternal life. For God did not send his Son into the world to condemn the world, but to save the world through him. (John 3:16–17)

> This is love: not that we loved God, but that he loved us and sent his Son as an atoning sacrifice for our sins. (1 John 4:10)

God loved the people of this world so much that He did something that appeared crazy. He didn't abandon the world; He invaded it. He didn't condemn the world; He saved it. God the Father sent God the Son to reach out to this fallen, sinful world to show just how much He loves us. God didn't ask us to try to reach up to Him. He became a man and reached out to us. The God who created the vastness of the universe with billions of galaxies, innumerable stars, and planets with His spoken word willfully limited Himself by becoming a man and living with the people He created and loves. Wow!

Just as amazing as this was two thousand years ago, it's still happening today. He is still reaching out to you. He is still calling you day after day, asking you to follow. If there is anything we can learn from the events of His arrival in Bethlehem, it is that Jesus is relentless, inexhaustible, and passionate in His pursuit of you. You can tell Him to quit calling. He won't. You can tell Him to leave you alone. He can't. He loves you too much to ever abandon you. You can try to ignore His calling, but He will eventually wear you down. Not even your past or current behavior can make Him stop calling. He has your number. You might as well pick up the phone.

If you have been avoiding Jesus as well as running, denying, or delaying, how about responding to Him today? He's not calling to make you feel guilty. He's calling to tell you how much He loves you, forgives you, and wants you to follow Him into a new future. You can try to resist longer, but know this: He will never stop reaching out to you.

Scripture for the Day:

Isaiah 65:1–2

Thought for the Day:

Since Jesus is never going to stop calling, how will you answer Him today? Respond and say, "Yes, Lord, here I am."

GOD'S GREATEST DESIRE IS YOU

What's your greatest desire? Is it finally getting your dream house, maybe going on a dream vacation, or possibly winning the lottery? Maybe it's tough even coming up with a "greatest desire." We all have many wants that may or may not be realized in this life. What would God's greatest desire be? He's the God who has everything anyway. What could He possibly desire? The answer is simple ... you. You are God's greatest desire. Read what He says about you:

> See what great love the Father has lavished on us, that we should be called children of God! And that is what we are! (1 John 3:1)

> The Spirit you received does not make you slaves, so that you live in fear again; rather, the Spirit you received brought about your adoption to sonship. And by him we cry, "Abba, Father." (Rom. 8:15)

The greatest desire of God's heart is to have a relationship with you. He doesn't simply want you to believe in Him. That's not relational. He doesn't simply want religious activities. That's rather cold. His greatest desire is you. His love is so incomprehensible that His greatest desire is for you to become part of His family, adopted as His son or daughter. God lavishes His love on us in a crazy manner in the hope that we will in turn love Him back. God's love for us is relentless because His longing for a relationship with us is relentless as well.

This is why when someone asked Jesus one day about what was the greatest activity someone could do for God, Jesus responded by saying that to love God was at the top of the list. It was a relational response. God's greatest desire is for a relationship. God's most earnest desire is for your love, not your religion, rules, or rituals. God's greatest desire is you.

I know we all have a tendency to think, *Surely God desires more than this. Certainly there is some great work or cause He would have us address in this life.* These aren't the things that light up a Father's heart. It is knowing your kids love you and want to spend time with you that satisfies a heart. God doesn't want or need more work out of you. What He desires is more of *you.*

If you struggle with believing you are important to God, maybe today is the day to stop using the world's standard for significance and adopt God's standard. You are made in His image, saved by His Son, indwelt by His Spirit, and adopted into His family. His greatest desire is simply for you. Even with all your flaws and inconsistencies, with all your past mistakes and regrets, God longs for you even more than the physical universe He created. Maybe today would be a great day to love Him back.

Scripture for the Day:

Mark 12:29–31

Thought for the Day:

Isaiah 49:16 says, "See, I have engraved you on the palms of my hands." Just think about being so valuable to God that your name is tattooed on His palms.

GOD CARES ABOUT YOU

Man, I hate being sick. Last week I was sicker than I have been in over thirty years. Sunday night it hit me suddenly, like a ton of bricks. Out of nowhere, I began having chills and a fever. By morning a full-blown case of strep throat assaulted my body. I won't go into too many details, but let's just say that I'd never seen tonsils look like that before. I'm not a squeamish kind of guy. I field-dress deer and elk, but what I saw in my throat wasn't natural. I'm convinced that strep isn't something you should get when you're fifty years old. Note to self! Even though I was on antibiotics by Monday afternoon, the strep still took me out of the game all week. This was the first time in my life I missed work all week.

So why do I share my strep throat woes with you? Because sometimes when life gets painful, whether it be a sickness or some other form of adverse circumstance, we can begin to question whether God really cares about us. I've had countless conversations with people over the years who are in the middle of some type of personal storm, and they struggle with believing God cares. They begin to question God's love for them.

We seem to have this tendency in our human nature to question God's goodness when we encounter pain. In these times we need to remember that our pain has a way of blurring our vision and distorting our reality. Why do we think God owes us a pain-free life? Why is it that when life gets dark, painful, and uncertain that we so quickly want to blame God? What is it about the brokenness of this life that makes us question God?

During the upbringing of my two daughters, my girls never blamed me or questioned my love for them when they got hurt—not even once! My oldest daughter once fractured her leg on a friend's trampoline. She didn't get mad at me. She didn't tell me I didn't care. A few years later she was in gymnastics class, and as she did a back handspring, she snapped her forearm. We hurried off and met her and the coach at the hospital. After the x-ray, the doctor explained to us that she needed surgery. She never looked at me and said, "This is your fault!" She never concluded that I didn't care. Not once did she doubt my love for her. Instead of withdrawing from me, we came together in a father-daughter way that goes beyond words. So why do we question God?

This broken world, and all the pain and discomfort that comes with it, should be a motivator for us to run *to* Jesus, not *away* from Him. It should cause us to realize just how much we need Him, not how much He doesn't care. We need to reject these false beliefs that get in the way and create barriers from Jesus about being our greatest source of strength, courage, and help in our time of need. Jesus never promised a pain-free ride, stress-free existence, or sickness-free experience. We shouldn't be surprised, then, when this life is hard. That doesn't indicate He doesn't care. It's quite the contrary. He cared so much that He died for us, placed His Spirit in us, adopted us into His family, and assures us of an eternity with Him.

If you're in the middle of a season of struggle, sickness, disappointment, stress, or relational turmoil, please don't conclude that your heavenly Father doesn't care. He loves you with an everlasting love. He cares deeply that you hurt. He sees every tear. He knows about every sleepless night. He understands every broken piece of your wounded heart. He may not remove the pain, but He will never remove His presence from you. Every good dad runs to his kids when they hurt. He may not be able to make the pain go away, but his presence makes the difference. God is right there with you, wanting to make the difference in your life. Don't allow your pain to distort just how much He loves you. He's right there … and yes, He cares.

> I will be glad and rejoice in your love, for you saw my
> affliction and knew the anguish of my soul. (Ps. 31:7)

Answer me, Lord, out of the goodness of your love; in your great mercy turn to me. (Ps. 69:16)

Then young women will dance and be glad, young men and old as well. I will turn their mourning into gladness; I will give them comfort and joy instead of sorrow. (Jer. 31:13)

Scripture for the Day:

John 3:16–17

Thought for the Day:

Have you struggled with believing God cares for you when life became difficult? What difficult issues are you facing today that give you an opportunity to run *to* God instead of *away from* Him?

WHEN LIFE MAKES NO SENSE

No matter who you are, there will be a time when life makes no sense. Circumstances will leave you bewildered, confused, wounded, and lonely. You got blindsided. You never saw that one coming. Where is God when life doesn't make sense? Where is God when the piece of the puzzle you were just handed seems too dark and ugly to fit into any plan? How can God use this one? You don't know what to do. You're paralyzed by fear and confusion. Your mind doesn't even have the ability to process them. Sometimes life makes no sense.

Years ago, I was on staff at a church for twelve years. I served as the youth pastor and then as the associate pastor, and I was being voted on to be the senior pastor. The church loved me, and I loved them. It seemed like a match God Himself had made ... or so I thought. Church policy required a 90 percent yes vote. Most attendees weren't official members. The 90 percent vote lacked only two votes. Later someone discovered that two people who lacked voting rights had cast those no votes.

Needless to say, this revelation caused church chaos. The denomination didn't support me and in fact asked me to immediately leave the premises. Therefore, the next day, after twelve years of service, I packed up my office and left for good. There were no good-byes or farewells. No closure. The church was in shambles, I was an emotional wreck, and it appeared that God was nowhere in sight. Since I was now unemployed and needed to provide for my family. I went to work for a friend and washed windows. I was out of the ministry, and it felt like I was out of the sight of God as well. This change made no sense at all.

When life makes no sense, it shakes us to the core of what we believe. It was during the time I spent washing windows that I had to answer some profound questions regarding God Himself. Let me share with you some of my conclusions, which helped guide me as I tried to follow Jesus through some of the most confusing times of my life. When life doesn't make sense, we must have some foundational beliefs that remain unchanged, regardless of the confusion. These beliefs become light in our darkness and lead us forward.

1. When life doesn't make sense, God is still good (Ps. 86:5).
2. When life doesn't make sense, God still profoundly loves me (Rom. 8:31–39).
3. When life doesn't make sense, God still believes in me (Ps. 37:23–24).
4. When life doesn't make sense, God is still faithful (1 Cor. 1:9).
5. When life doesn't make sense, God still has plans for my life (Jer. 29:11).
6. When life doesn't make sense, obedience still matters (James 1:25).
7. When life doesn't make sense, humbly accept the circumstances (James 4:10).

No matter what is going on in your life right now, these things are true. The circumstances cannot change who God is and what His word says about you. When life doesn't make sense, we must cling to the unchanging truths of God's word. It is His truth that is an anchor in the dark storms of our lives. There comes a time when we stop believing what we feel and choose to believe the unchanging truths of God's word. If you are in a season where life just doesn't make sense, I am truly sorry. I know it is confusing, painful, and dark; but God hasn't abandoned you. I know you don't see or feel Him, but He is there right beside you. The light will come back. The dawn will break. The heaviness will be lifted. Whatever the circumstances are, they may never make sense to you. It's not about understanding; it's about following. Just choose to follow Him today.

Scripture for the Day:

Look up and reflect on the scriptures given for each truth.

Thought for the Day:

Reflect on the seven provided statements and ask yourself whether you truly believe these truths, even though life doesn't make any sense.

RUNNING FROM GOD

There's a story in the Bible about a prophet named Jonah. God gave him a very specific assignment and message for the people of Nineveh. Instead of following God's instructions, he went in the opposite direction toward the Mediterranean Sea, got on a boat, and did his best to run from God. The only problem with his ingenious plan was, how does one run from God?

Now that his plan worked to perfection, he fell fast asleep in the bottom of the ship. On deck, though, the sailors became worried. The sky turned black, the waves grew larger, and the wind howled through the sails. They were now in for the fight of their lives. As conditions worsened, they threw cargo over the sides to lighten the load. Finally, someone went down in the ship to find Jonah. There he was, fast asleep and still dreaming about how he had pulled one over on God. When a terrified sailor woke him, the gravity of the situation began to sink in. "This storm is for me!" The weather forecast was for clear sailing. The storm wasn't just a coincidence. *I guess my plan didn't work as well as I had hoped.* "Okay, God … You have my attention!"

You may be familiar with this story and its outcome. Maybe you've never read this story before. If this describes you, then let me encourage you to go to the book of Jonah and read how the story ends for yourself. There are other lessons from this story besides the one I want to address here. What's the lesson from the brief part of the story I shared? If we run from God, we should expect a storm.

Sometimes we can overemphasize certain character traits of God. We love to talk about God's love, mercy, forgiveness, and grace. I love writing about these wonderful truths about God as well. But if we're not careful, we can ignore other qualities that are equally important. Like what? We can ignore the accountability of God. Even though God unconditionally loves us, there is still accountability in this relationship. Following Jesus comes with a very basic understanding; we follow Jesus. If we choose to go in the exact opposite direction, we should expect a storm. We should expect consequences. Running away from God in any area of our lives won't bring blessing. He loves us way too much for this.

Hebrews 12:10–11 says, "They disciplined us for a little while as they thought best; but God disciplines us for our good, in order that we may share in his holiness. No discipline seems pleasant at the time, but painful. Later on, however, it produces a harvest of righteousness and peace for those who have been trained by it."

Running from God will always bring God's loving hand of discipline. Yes, He may actually tailor-make a storm just for us. We may think we're getting away with something. We know what God is calling us to do. We know what God is asking us to stop doing, but we go in the opposite direction anyway. Then the skies get dark, the waves get big, and the wind of circumstances begins to howl. What's going on? Running from God brings a storm.

Not every storm in life is the result of our running from God. Sometimes storms are simply part of living in this broken world. They're just part of navigating in the turbulent sea of life. But other times storms are the result of choosing to ignore what God has plainly said. When we choose a course we know is in direct violation of what God wants from us, we should expect accountability. Why? Because He loves us. We discipline our children because we love them. We hold them accountable because we know it's good for them and their development of character. Why, then, are we so surprised when God does the same with us? He wants us to share in His holiness. He wants us to resemble Him.

If life is turbulent right now, maybe it's a good time to do some self-evaluation. When life gets tough, it's an opportune time to ask God,

"Lord, is this storm from You? Do you want my attention?" Remember, not every storm is because we're running from God. It's quite possible, though you already know the answer to this question. Yes, you have been running, and yes, God does want your attention. His grace will be sufficient for you. His mercy is boundless. His forgiveness will be yours in abundance. His love for you is still as passionate as it ever has been. What He simply wants is you. He wants you to trust Him. Now, will you run back to Him?

Scripture for the Day:

Hebrews 12:4–13

Thought for the Day:

Our daily struggling with sin is very different from choosing a path away from Jesus. We will all battle our fleshly desires until the day we die. Focus rather on the areas where you have given up and walked away from what Jesus would have you do.

OUR HOPE IN FAILURE

I hate to fail. I despise losing. My competitive personality simply has a hard time with this entire concept. As a kid playing sports, losing was unacceptable. If we didn't win or perform at my best, I was brutal on myself. Sometimes it would take me days to get over a defeat. I don't know where this intensity for winning came from. It just seemed to always be part of my DNA. My sports days are long gone, but my intensity for winning is still part of my personality. I still hate losing, but now I get over it a lot faster. I've come to accept the fact that losing and failing are simply realities of this life. Failure is a common thread of our fallen humanity. I fail all the time. You fail all the time. What do I mean? As much as I want to follow Jesus in obedience, I fall short often. To put it bluntly, I fail.

Where is our hope when we fail spiritually, relationally, morally, and in every other way we can imagine? Many people I've talked to over the years put their hope in a variety of hopeless places. Let's just face it— Christians have a hard time dealing with their own failings. Because of this difficulty, they put their hope in denial: "Let's just pretend we don't fail." They put their hope in effort: "Next time I will try twice as hard." They put their hope in performance: "Look at all the progress I've made." They put their hope in comparisons: "I'm not as bad as they are." Because these strategies never work long term, people often lose hope altogether. They conclude they are "losers" because they lose constantly in their relationship with God. Many Christians conclude that there must be something wrong with them because they simply can't spiritually perform well enough. "Why do I keep doing things I don't want to do?" The apostle Paul asked the same question. Here is what he concluded:

Romans 7:21–25 says, "So I find this law at work: Although I want to do good, evil is right there with me. For in my inner being I delight in

God's law; but I see another law at work in me, waging war against the law of my mind and making me a prisoner of the law of sin at work within me. What a wretched man I am! Who will rescue me from this body that is subject to death? Thanks be to God, who delivers me through Jesus Christ our Lord!"

If you read the verses leading up to this passage, you'll see that Paul talked about his ongoing struggle with sin. Sometimes he wanted to do what was right, but he ended up doing what was wrong anyway. Just because we gave our lives to Jesus doesn't mean we end up living sinless lives. Our fallen humanity and struggle with sin will always be part of our human existence in this life. They never go away. Sometimes we emotionally feel just like Paul. We feel wretched! We feel defeated. So where is our hope? Many people look at the last phrase in this passage, focus on "who delivers me through Jesus Christ," and assume this means performance. We are delivered from our ongoing failure to sin. Really? Is that your experience? If our hope is going to be placed in not sinning, we're all in big trouble. When was the last time you had a sinless week or even a sinless day? I rest my case. If this is where our hope is found, we are all truly hopeless.

Our deliverance from sin isn't in being sinless but in finding the provision Jesus made for us through His death and resurrection. This is why on the heels of Romans 7 there is Romans 8:1: "Therefore, there is now no condemnation for those who are in Christ Jesus." The real deliverance isn't being condemned, because we still struggle with sin. The real hope is that God through Jesus completely accepts us, despite our ongoing struggles and failures. Our hope has nothing to do with us or our spiritual performance; it has everything to do with Jesus.

The point is this: you're not a spiritual loser. Struggling with our sinful tendencies will always be part of our humanity in this life. There will be days when we do well and days when we struggle. Stop beating yourself up because you failed yet again. Jesus has this covered. Jesus still accepts you just as much when you win as when you fail. Provision for all your sin has been made. Provision for sins you have yet to commit has already been made. Our hope is in the unconditional acceptance of Jesus, not in the things we do. This doesn't give us excuses for our sin. This simply recognizes the provision for our sin and the reality of our ongoing struggles.

If you've been allowing your failure to define your relationship with God, get your eyes off your performance and focus on the person of Jesus. He has you covered. He is your source of hope in failure.

Scripture for the Day:

Romans 7:14–8:1

Thought for the Day:

Spend some time thinking about your relationship with God and what defines it. Does your performance define it? Does your failure or success define it? Does Jesus define it?

YOU ARE GOD'S HANDIWORK

For years I struggled with the role of being a pastor. I remember being a youth pastor years ago, yet I would never allow anyone to call me the "pastor." I asked everyone to call me the "youth director." One reason I struggled so much was that I just didn't fit the mold. I looked at other pastors and knew I was certainly not like them. I didn't talk like them, act like them, think like them, or dress like them; I didn't go to the right schools like them or even like their leisure activities, such as golf. Apparently, pastors are supposed to play golf (I hate golf, by the way). I just didn't fit in.

I remember asking God, "Why on earth do You want me to be a pastor? I'm just a small-town farm kid who would have been happy with a simple small-town life." There was a time when I finally accepted that God knew best. He never wanted me to "fit in." He hadn't designed me to be a clone or a follower of the masses. He wanted me to stop comparing myself to others and concluding that there was something wrong with me. He wanted me to keep my eyes on Him and believe He had made me unique for His purposes. When I finally believed this, I started letting people call me "pastor."

Ephesians. 2:10 says, "For we are God's handiwork, created in Christ Jesus to do good works, which God prepared in advance for us to do." This verse applies not only to me but to you, too. You are God's handiwork. You aren't a mistake, an error, or a mishap; you aren't faulty, incomplete, or defective in any manner. You are God's handiwork. He made you just the way you are. He gave you your unique gifts, passions, personality, talents, and enormous potential that only He knows. He created you uniquely for a unique purpose. He created you in Christ Jesus to do good works, which God prepared in advance for you to do. Wow. In eternity past, God knew you would be born at this precise point in history for such a time as this. He designed you not to fit in but for His purposes. He didn't create you to follow the crowd but to be distinct and set apart from the crowd. There are things only you can do, because God made you this way. God put more inside you than you have any capacity to understand. You aren't who you think you are. You are who God created you to be.

Maybe it's time to stop listening to all the other voices and hear the voice of the One who created you. Everyone has an opinion of who you need to be. The media, your friends, and your family have an opinion, and so does your employer. Could it be that the huge void you feel inside your very soul is the absence of *you*? It's the absence of you being and living in the manner God created you to exist. Out of all the important information one can discover in this life, discovering how God uniquely designed you should be somewhere at the top of that list. Until you discover, accept, and live out this design, something will always be missing. When I finally stopped resisting who I was designed to be and finally embraced it, my life was liberated. I was free to be a "different" pastor, one who doesn't like to golf or do a host of other things. I was free to look at my role in a unique way and follow God's unique path. It was the one He had prepared for me millions of years ago. You are His handiwork as well. Isn't it time to stop being someone else's handiwork and start becoming God's?

Scripture for the Day:

1 Corinthians 12:1–31

Thought for the Day:

Do you struggle with who you are? It's difficult to accept the truth that you are God's handiwork? Do you feel that you live the expectations of others rather than what God desires for you? What can you do to begin to embrace living in a way that resembles God's handiwork?

DON'T LET YOUR FAITH FAIL

Failure is simply part of the human experience. I'm not here trying to make excuses for our shortcomings, faults, flaws, and brokenness; but the reality is that these issues are simply never going away in this life. The problem arises in us when we become obsessed with our failures. Let's face it; it's rather hard not to be. In our hearts we truly want to follow Jesus, and yet our behavior seems to fall so short. We want to do what's right, and yet we lose our temper on the freeway ... again. We truly love our spouse, and yet we said something we regret ... again. We want our thoughts to be pure, but the Internet ambushed us yet again, and there went those pure thoughts right out the mental window. We know we're not supposed to love the world, and yet here we are, pursuing a life of materialism. We know we need to be humble, yet here is pride rising up inside us, hindering or hurting another person we love ... yet again! What's wrong with us? It's the same condition that plagues every human on earth; we are *all* marred by sin.

Before you sink into despair, let's focus on the good news. I know you're thinking, *What good news?* Jesus! Jesus is the good news. He isn't obsessed with all our specific individual failures as we are. He takes a much more holistic view of who we are. He knows we are going to fail often in this life. Even after we give our lives to Jesus, our behavior, attitudes, and motives are far from perfect. That's why He died on a cross. He paid the penalty for our sin so we will be perfect in eternity someday. Until then, His righteousness covers us. His righteousness is applied to us. My righteousness on my best day is still nothing but filthy rags, according to God's word. This makes Jesus much more concerned about our overall faith than our individual failures.

Let me summarize a great story from God's word that illustrates this truth. Jesus had His last meal with His disciples hours before His crucifixion. They all declared their undying loyalty to Jesus, even to their death. Jesus knew what was coming. His entire disciple team was going to crash and burn in an epic failure in only a few hours. Of course, Peter was the most vocal of the bunch. Jesus looked straight at him, knowing full well that in a few hours Simon Peter would deny he even knew Jesus. He said, "Simon, Simon, Satan has asked to sift all of you as wheat. But I have prayed for you, Simon, that your faith may not fail. And when you have turned back, strengthen your brothers" (Luke 22:31–32).

You know what bothers me about this response to Peter? If Jesus knew Satan was going to come after His friend, why did He not pray that Peter wouldn't fail? Why didn't He pray that Peter would win? Why didn't He pray for overwhelming victory? Why not pray for Peter to bring the smack down on Satan? That's what we would have done. Instead, notice that He pleaded in prayer that "your faith should not fail." He didn't obsess over the fact that Peter would deny Him. Instead, He prayed that even in failure, His faith wouldn't fail. To me this is absolutely fascinating. Jesus was much more concerned with Peter's overall faith than with his individual failure. It was like Jesus said to Peter, "Listen, Peter, you're going to lose this fight, but don't lose your faith over it. I still believe in you."

What a great principle for us. I have seen many believers in Jesus lose their faith because they lost their fight with sin. Our brokenness simply doesn't disappear the moment we give our lives to Jesus. The struggle with sin is our battle while we live in this world. It is *never* going away in this life. Some issues are ingrained through years of repetition. Some have generational reinforcements that span decades. Some may be weaknesses that come from our personalities, environments, or even past trauma. There are days when we rise above these issues. There are other days when we feel sifted like wheat, and we lay beaten, wounded, and defeated by sin yet again. We desperately need to hear the voice of Jesus saying, "Hey, I know Satan took you down this time and you didn't win this fight, but don't lose your faith over it. I still believe in you."

If you've been feeling defeated lately, which is causing your faith to waver, take heart. Jesus isn't surprised by your struggle, nor is He obsessed by the specifics of it. He knows full well that this life will be filled with failed attempts to follow Him. What He is much more concerned about is that your faith in Him doesn't fail. Why would He be more concerned with this? Because your faith in Him is your only chance at any type of victory in this life. Your relationship with Jesus isn't based on your performance. It's not determined by your victories. It is His unconditional, compassionate, and never-ending love for you that gives you the strength to stand up yet again. This is why Jesus prayed the way He did. Our failures can cause us to give up on God, but they never cause God to give up on us. As long as our faith doesn't fail, we will always go back to Jesus, fall into His arms, be embraced by His compassionate love, and hear His tender voice telling us to try again. "Don't lose your faith over this failure. I still believe in you."

Scripture for the Day:

Ephesians 3:14–19

Thought for the Day:

Does your performance or Jesus' incomprehensible love for you define your relationship with Him? One perspective can cause your faith to waver, while the other becomes an unshakable foundation.

CHAPTER 3

FOLLOWING JESUS PRACTICALLY

LOVING GOD WITH ALL YOUR SOUL

When we hear the word *soul*, we have all kinds of mental images and meanings. What comes to your mind when you hear this word? *Soul* can mean the inner, immaterial part of humanity that exists after we die. Yet it can also refer to a description of a musician playing "soul" music. How does the Bible describe this word? The Bible describes the soul as representing your entire inner life. Your soul is everything you feel, decide, believe, think, choose, want, dwell on, turn to, and pursue. The soul is about what makes you happy, what fills you with joy, where your sorrow and sadness lie, and what gives you peace. *Your soul is the basis of your personality and what makes you, you.*

Now remember: Jesus said we should love God with all our souls (Mark 12:30). You're thinking, *Wow, that's pretty comprehensive.* That's true. To love God with all your soul is to love God with everything internal. We should love God with all our emotions, desires, and unique personalities; all that makes us who we are. To love God with all our souls means we first allow Him to transform our souls. We expose our entire inner selves to Him. Then we uniquely express our love to Him from this place.

For example, my inner soul is a type A, a highly driven, goal-oriented, very passionate personality. My soul likes taking risks, needs adventure, and seeks close friendships to experience this journey together. I need to let God transform my soul and then love God from that transformed soul. I love God by being passionate for Him, being driven by His agenda, taking risks for His kingdom, and enjoying sweet friendships with other believers as we take on an adventure together. Being the lead pastor of Foothills and fulfilling this responsibility out of whom God made me to be are how I love God with my soul.

But loving God with my soul doesn't always have to be about serving and ministry. I love to hunt, fish, camp in the wilderness, travel internationally, experience new exciting cultures, and meet new people. When I find great joy in these activities, I am living in the way God created my soul to thrive. In these moments, I love Him out of my personality. I love God with my soul. When I live my life in a manner consistent with the way He made my soul breathe, there is a deep connection and love I have with God.

Does your inner life love God? Does your personality love God? Do your affections love God? Are you living in a way that your soul can breathe and find its true expression? Have you allowed Him to transform your inner self so you can love God from the depths of your soul? We are asked to love God not only with all our hearts but also with all our souls. How can you love God from your soul today?

Scripture for the Day:

Psalm 139

Thought for the Day:

Being who God created you to be brings Him pleasure. How can you love God out of the uniqueness of the personality He created in you?

CONSISTENCY

Doing the right things consistently isn't easy. We see the benefit of right choices only as we work at being consistent. Choosing the right action once doesn't usually have much of a payoff. Don't you wish eating one healthy meal a month was enough to be healthy? Wouldn't it be nice if only two times a month in the gym were enough to achieve great health and stamina? How amazing would it be to go to work only one day and be paid for a full week? We all know this is fantasy. To experience the benefit from anything good we choose to do, we have to be committed to consistency.

Our relationship with God works off the same principle. The Bible is filled with tremendous promises every believer can experience in this life. So what's the problem? Consistency. Many followers of Jesus expect great results from their faith with very little consistency. It would be like expecting immediate physical results by going to the gym once a month. It just doesn't work like that. Consistency will chart the course of our lives. Whatever we are consistent with will determine what we will experience, good or bad. Therefore, if we desire to grow in our relationship with God, we must decide to grow in our consistency with the things that help foster this relationship. Below are six areas to focus on, with the resulting blessing of consistency:

- Consistent obedience to God will result in experiencing consistent blessing from God.
- Consistent learning of spiritual truth will result in experiencing consistent spiritual growth.
- Consistent loving relationships with others will result in experiencing consistent love and encouragement from others.
- Consistent generosity to God will result in experiencing consistent provision from God.

- Consistent service for God will result in experiencing consistent impact and influence for the kingdom of God.
- Consistent prayer to God will result in experiencing consistent results and answers from God.

Please understand that consistent doesn't mean perfect. Perfection is impossible in this life. I love how Proverbs 24:16 says it. "For though the righteous fall seven times, they rise again." Often we see consistency in our lives by our simply refusing to quit, to throw in the towel, and to conclude that consistency doesn't pay off. Consistency means that when I fail I will always get back up and try again.

Hebrews 5:14 says, "But solid food is for the mature, *who by constant use* have trained themselves to distinguish good from evil" (emphasis added). Did you notice that? It is by "constant use"—in other words, consistency. Consistency created yet another good result. Spiritual consistency is a powerful thing and is an irreplaceable quality for the follower of Jesus.

My guess is that you struggle with being consistent. I bet you struggle with reading your Bible, praying, serving, being obedient, and growing as a follower of Jesus. Why would I say this? Because at times I struggle with these things too. The best choice we can all make to help us grow in consistency is to decide right now never to give up. If you're discouraged and disappointed in your lack of consistency and progress, it's time to get back up and try again. Just making the decision to try again is growth in consistency. Stop listening to that voice that tells you it's worthless. Refuse to listen to the voice that tells you you'll never change. That voice is lying to you. The spirit behind that voice wants to keep you a prisoner. The blessings of consistently following Jesus are yours. You are a child of God. You are His son or daughter. You belong to Him. Now, simply get up and try again. Do you hear that other voice? It's Jesus saying, "Here I am. Take My hand. Let's do this together!"

Scripture for the Day:

Philippians 4:13

Thought for the Day:

Give your inconsistency to Jesus today. Acknowledge that only by His power and strength can you grow in consistency. Remember, Jesus is here to help you today, not condemn you.

CONSISTENT OBEDIENCE

I have glaucoma. The elevated pressure level in my right eye has caused the optic nerve to deteriorate 50 percent. That's right, I have only half of it left. To protect what remains, I have to take two different types of eye drops to relieve this pressure. I take a specific type of drop in the morning and a different type in the evening every day. Notice I said "every day." I take them with me when I'm on vacation, when I'm camping, when I'm elk hunting, and when I'm on mission trips. It doesn't matter where I am or where I go; these drops come with me. You see, if I want to keep my vision, I need to take these drops consistently for the rest of my life. Applying them once in a while isn't going to protect my eye.

This needs to be our mind-set when it comes to obediently following Jesus. If I want to experience the blessings that result from obeying God's word, I need to make up my mind to consistently follow it. Following it occasionally, once in a while, or when I feel like it won't give me the blessing it promises. We don't experience all the promises from the word of God simply by hearing it or mentally knowing it. We must follow it to be blessed.

> Blessed rather are those who hear the word of God and obey it. (Luke 11:28)

> But whoever looks intently into the perfect law that gives freedom, and continues in it—not forgetting what they have heard, but doing it—they will be blessed in what they do. (James 1:25)

Surveys reveal that Americans who consider themselves Christians aren't convinced that God's word should be completely followed. Only 46 percent of Christians believe in any absolute moral truth. If over half of believers don't believe God's word is absolute moral truth, it's no wonder there is such great inconsistency. It's no wonder followers tend to pick and choose rather than submit their lives to obey what the Bible teaches. They don't view God's word like I view my eye drops. Just as my eye drops are absolutely essential for me to see, obedience to God's word is absolutely essential for life.

If you truly want to see the blessing that results from obedience to the word of God, you're going to have to be consistent. Occasional obedience isn't going to get it done. Obedience has to become a lifestyle. Don't say that you tried God's word for a while and it didn't work. That would be like my saying I tried my eye drops for a week and they didn't work. I want my vision to be blessed for the rest of my life. Therefore, I submit my will to taking eye drops for the rest of my life. Do you want your life to be blessed? Then decide to submit your will to obedience to the word of God for the rest of your life. Why don't you "taste and see" for yourself?

Ps. 34:8 "Taste and see that the Lord is good; blessed is the one who takes refuge in him."

God loves to prove Himself to people. Why not give Him the opportunity to amaze you with what His word can do in your life?

Scripture for the Day:

2 Timothy 3:16

Thought for the Day:

How deep is your conviction that the Bible is God's absolute moral truth for you? What causes you to struggle with this conviction? Is this one of the reasons you struggle with following it consistently?

BELIEVING OR CHOOSING

As a pastor for more than thirty years, I have had many conversations with people who struggle with believing that the truths in God's word have life-changing power. Often I have listened to people say something like, "I tried that once, and it didn't work for me" or, "I went to church years ago, but I didn't see any relevance." Maybe even, "I've read the Bible before, but it didn't do anything for me." I realize there are many barriers people have to work through before there is some type of authentic spiritual connection, but I want to address only one. There is one obstacle I see in so many people's lives that keep them from experiencing all the power and promises of God's word. It is the difference between simply believing and choosing. Maybe today you're struggling with accepting the truth that change is actually possible. Maybe it's difficult embracing the fact that the promises of God are for you to experience. It could be the difference between believing and choosing.

In our western culture we are influenced most by how we think and what we believe. Our intellects are the driving force behind our beliefs. Therefore, when the Bible tells us to believe something, we conclude that this is merely an intellectual exercise whereby we simply agree with the word of God. Since I agree with the word of God, therefore, what the word of God promises should now be my reality. I have intellectually agreed, and now the promises of God should be mine in all their fullness. The dilemma comes when nothing happens. What's wrong? Maybe God's word doesn't work. Unfortunately, many draw this erroneous conclusion.

When the Bible talks about "believing," it is so much more than merely an intellectual exercise. To truly believe is to choose. To truly believe is to take action. To believe the word of God isn't simply mentally agreeing with a list of beliefs. These beliefs should radically alter your life. I can mentally agree that the Boeing 737 will safely take me to my destination, but until I get on that plane, I don't truly believe. When the Bible talks about believing, it requires you to choose.

Years ago I used to take students to ropes courses. Many of the events were thirty-five to forty feet in the air. If you had any misgiving about heights, you were sure to experience all your feelings had to offer—on steroids. Now, mind you, everyone was completely safe. Each person wore a harness and helmet, and someone always had a hold of the rope. It was a great exercise on choosing to put your beliefs into action. Did everyone mentally agree he or she was safe? Yes. If you looked at all the safety equipment involved, it seemed pretty safe. But as soon as you stand on a log suspended forty feet in the air, now it is time to see whether your beliefs are real. I saw fear completely paralyze some kids. All they had was an intellectual agreement to safety. When you're forty feet in the air, your mental agreement just doesn't get it done. Unfortunately, many people live their faith just like this. This is why it doesn't work for them. This type of faith doesn't work for anyone.

If you've been struggling with this issue, the best thing you can do is take a step out on the log. Put your faith into action. Trust what God says in His word. Do what He is asking you to do. The power and promises of God are waiting for you on the other side of your choice, not on the other side of your belief. God blesses the actions of faith, not the faith by itself. It's time to choose, not simply believe. James 1:25 says, "But whoever looks intently into the perfect law that gives freedom, and continues in it—not forgetting what they have heard, but doing it—they will be blessed in what they do."

Scripture for the Day:

James 2:14–26

Thought for the Day:

How many truths from God's word are left in neutral, having no power in your life because you have yet to act on them?

DO YOU FOLLOW THE RIGHT GPS?

So much of our technology today has a built-in GPS. There is one in our smartphones. Almost all our new vehicles come with a GPS as standard equipment. My fish finder on my boat even has a GPS as part of the system. Being able to find our way effectively and efficiently is a pretty big deal in our society. Some people have put so much trust in their GPS that they have driven into ponds and lakes, and taken gravel roads into a wilderness, only to be hopelessly lost. Certainly the GPS can't be wrong, can it?

God has given mankind His GPS to navigate this life. God's word is "God's Positioning System" (GPS). If we desire to navigate this life successfully, we will need to rely on something besides ourselves. Just as in the case of our technology, our senses and feelings don't always do a good job of determining direction. So it is true when it comes to navigating this life. Trusting in our feelings can often lead us astray. We need a more objective standard to guide our lives. This is why God has given us His word. Too many people look at the word of God as simply good moral teaching instead of the absolute standard for navigating this life. Just look at how God's word is described.

> Your word is a lamp for my feet, a light on my path. (Ps. 119:105)

> The unfolding of your words gives light; it gives understanding to the simple. (Ps. 119:130)

> Direct my footsteps according to your word; let no sin rule over me. (Ps. 119:133)

> The statutes you have laid down are righteous; they are fully trustworthy. (Ps. 119:138)

Are you using God's GPS for your life? Are you making decisions and setting the direction of your life by using His word? Do you realize this is why He gave it to us? God gave us a life map by which to chart the course of our lives in this dark, broken, and confusing world. You don't need to be smart enough to figure out how to navigate. You can follow His word. The word of God will show you how to navigate relationships, marriage, and parenting; and how to experience joy, satisfaction, and hope. God's word will guide your steps when you have no idea which direction to choose. Are you trusting God's word with your life? This is why it was given to us.

A GPS doesn't do us any good if we ignore its directions or don't even turn it on. God's word works the same way. If we never read it and ignore it when we do, it will have no navigating power in our lives. Aren't you tired of feeling lost? God has given you a priceless navigational tool. Isn't it time you start using it?

Scripture for the Day:

Psalm 119

Thought for the Day:

Reflect on how Psalm 119 describes the word of God. What keeps you from experiencing the word of God like the author?

THERE IS A SPIRITUAL COVER-UP GOING ON

It seems like there is always another scandal, another exposed cover-up, in the news these days. Whether it has something to do with Wall Street, a prominent political figure, or even an athlete, something eventually gets exposed, and the truth finally comes to light. It seems there is no shortage of people hiding or masquerading as something they are not. Just last week someone called my dad on the phone, pretending to be his distraught grandson who needed money because he was in jail for a drug-possession charge. This is laughable because my dad and his grandson are very close. He knew better. His grandson is a follower of Jesus and wouldn't be in jail for such a crime. It was a scam, of course. It didn't work because my dad knew the truth.

There is a spiritual cover-up that's been going on since the beginning of time. As followers of Jesus, we face a spiritual enemy who wants to keep people from knowing and following the truth. As long as people are kept in the dark, he can take advantage of them. The Bible is very clear that Satan and his demons are real, and their activity is very real. There are two very specific motives of Satan we need to be aware of so we don't fall for his scams.

The first is that Satan wants to keep people blinded to the truth. Second Corinthians 4:4 says, "The god of this age has blinded the minds of unbelievers, so that they cannot see the light of the gospel that displays the glory of Christ, who is the image of God."

Spiritual blindness can happen in so many different ways. Sometimes we're blinded by ignorance, we are uninformed, or we simply have no idea there is another way to look at life. Often the enemy blinds us by orchestrating events to keep us busy and distracted. Our previous bad experiences with the church can blind us. Religion, rules, and rituals blind us. Sometimes the pain of relationships can blind us from seeing what God has for us. The disappointments of life can blind us to God's goodness and His truth. How can God be good when my life hurts so much? The last thing Satan wants you to see is the truth.

The second motive is that Satan wants to deceive people from believing the truth. John 8:44 says, "You belong to your father, the devil, and you want to carry out your father's desires. He was a murderer from the beginning, not holding to the truth, for there is no truth in him. When he lies, he speaks his native language, for he is a liar and the father of lies."

Satan not only wants to keep you blind to the truth; he introduces an alternative to the truth. For every truth God has for your life, Satan has a false imitation. I bet you've heard some of these lies: "All truth is relative," "All roads lead to God," "Whatever you do is okay as long as you're sincere," "God helps those who help themselves," "God just wants you to be happy," and "It feels so right; it can't be wrong." These simply represent a few common imitations. His false alternatives are limitless.

If we allow ourselves to be blinded and lied to, we will be scammed for the rest of our lives. An enemy in this world will continually take advantage of us. What can we do? Be committed to the truth. Where is the truth found? It is discovered in God's word. Second Timothy 3:16–17 says, *"All Scripture is God-breathed and is useful for teaching, rebuking, correcting and training in righteousness,* so that the servant of God may be thoroughly equipped for every good work" (emphasis added).

I don't believe most followers of Jesus realize what they have at their disposal. You have been given a tremendous gift called the Bible. It is your source of truth to expose the blindness and lies of the enemy. You don't need to put up with being scammed. Discipline yourself to read it, study it, and, most important, follow it. Let God's word change how you think. Allow the word of God to help you draw different conclusions about your life. Wear it as a set of glasses that help you interpret the world around you. Become a lover of the word of God. If you will, you will experience the liberation godly truth will bring to your life. Jesus said, "If we know the truth, the truth will set us free." It's time for you to experience this truth for yourself.

Scripture for the Day:

Psalm 119

Thought for the Day:

What is your opinion of the Bible? Do you believe the word of God is the ultimate truth for living this life or just another option to consider? Reflect on how the author of Psalm 119 looked at God's word.

NOT JUST MENTAL AGREEMENT

We give mental agreement to all kinds of things these days. When you sign on to free Wi-Fi, you have to click the "Do you agree?" box before gaining access. When you get a loan, you sign at the bottom that you accept all the terms and conditions (although no one really reads all that fine print). When you go to the doctor, you fill out the medical history form and then sign the waiver at the bottom. We constantly give mental agreement to things in our culture. The dilemma happens when we treat our relationship with Jesus like this. He becomes just another issue I have given mental agreement to. "Do you agree?" Check "yes."

"What's wrong with this?" you may ask. Everything! We have diminished faith to simply a belief system. We have reduced faith to a list of mental boxes we have checked off, and now "we're saved." We have made our experience with Jesus in this life merely mental agreement to doctrine instead of following a living, dynamic Person. We've made following Jesus into a contract we signed, but then we give very little thought to what it really means in our daily lives.

Many surveys today study why people are leaving the church across the country. Much of the research isn't very promising. Eight to ten thousand churches will close their doors this year. Large percentages of those in the twenty-five-and-younger category see no point in the church at all. Most people no longer associate church with experiencing God. It's apparent that "contract Christianity" isn't working very well. Jesus never asked people to check the box if they believe. He called people to radically follow Him. Luke 9:23–25 says, "Then he said to them all: 'Whoever wants to be my disciple must deny themselves and take up their cross daily and follow me. For whoever wants to save their life will lose it, but whoever loses their life for me will save it. What good is it for someone to gain the whole world, and yet lose or forfeit their very self?'"

This doesn't sound like simple mental agreement. This sounds like something that alters the very course of our lives. Biblical Christianity isn't simply believing that Jesus lived, died for our sins, and rose from the dead. Don't get me wrong; these are pretty important truths to agree to, but wouldn't Satan and all his demons agree to the same truths? What makes us different? We follow Jesus.

If you want to experience the risen Jesus, you must choose not only to believe in Him but also to follow Him. Experiencing Jesus in this life, in real time and in our real circumstances, requires us to follow Him, not just check a box that we agree. Genuine Christianity is where we follow Him; He doesn't follow us. Do you want to experience Jesus? Do you want to see Him in your life? Do you want to sense His presence? Would you like to see His power in you as your reality? If so, then you must choose to follow Him. "Whoever wants to be my disciple must deny themselves and take up their cross daily and follow me." (Matt. 16:24). This is how Jesus defined it. I think it is time to get back to His definition.

How about you? Are you struggling in your faith? Are you wondering, *What's the point?* Maybe you only have a mental agreement. Jesus is waiting to show you who He really is. He's waiting to invade your life and your struggles. He's waiting to show you He is so much more than a checkmark in a mental box. He's real, and He's calling you to follow Him. Now, what will you do?

Scripture for the Day:

Luke 9:23–25, Spend some extra time thinking about what these verses mean to you.

Thought for the Day:

Spend some time thinking about your faith journey. Is your faith more of a mental agreement to specific biblical truths, or is it more about following Jesus? How do you think Jesus is calling you to make some changes?

SPIRITUAL ATROPHY

I like to work out and be in shape. As I have gotten older, the need for exercise has only increased. Since I love the outdoors with all the fishing, hiking, and hunting, being in shape allows me to fully enjoy these activities. It just requires a certain level of physical endurance to reel in a three-hundred-pound sturgeon or pack out an elk on your back. The sad reality is how quickly I can begin to slip out of shape. Sometimes I will take several weeks off from the gym when my wife and I go on vacation. I believe the break is good for my body, but when I go back to the gym, oh my, am I sore for a week. It always amazes me how quickly my physical body can lose what I worked so hard to gain. God made our muscles to respond to exercise. Stop the exercise for an extended period of time, and atrophy sets in.

What is true physically is true spiritually as well. Our faith is designed to be exercised. If we use it, we grow our faith. If we don't exercise it, our faith diminishes and gets weaker. The fallacy that I see so many believers embrace is that after growing to a certain level of faith, they stop working it out, thinking they can maintain that level by inactivity. Not true. Faith is like a muscle. Use it or lose it. Faith isn't an intellectual thing, no more than working out physically is an intellectual thing. Both require activity, sweat, and effort.

> For physical training is of some value, but godliness has value for all things, holding promise for both the present life and the life to come. (1 Tim. 4:8)

> Therefore, my dear friends, as you have always obeyed—not only in my presence, but now much more in my absence—continue to work out your salvation with fear and trembling, for it is God who works in you

to will and to act in order to fulfill his good purpose.
(Phil. 2:12–13)

As a follower of Jesus, it should be your desire to have your faith strong.
How do you cooperate with Jesus, who is growing your faith? How do
you use it? How do you work it out? How do you begin to develop some
spiritual muscle? What things help you increase your spiritual stamina?
These are all great questions that require more time than I have here,
but let me give you some suggestions to get you on your way.

1. Follow what God's word says, and don't just *know* what God's
    word says. Following is hard, but knowing is easy. Will you
    follow what God's word says regarding relationships, marriage,
    finances, materialism, priorities, love and service, to name a
    few? Knowing doesn't equate to spiritual maturity; following
    does. If you aren't working hard at following, you're not
    working out.

2. Rely on Jesus to help you follow. The reason most people
    don't rely on Jesus is because they're not trying to follow Jesus.
    They're not working out spiritually. When you begin to follow
    Jesus, you soon realize you cannot do this without His help. It
    forces you to learn how to rely on Him. He is the best spiritual
    trainer there is. He will help your faith grow and develop. Ask
    Him for His help. Ask Him for the desire and power to do
    what pleases Him.

3. Serve the needs of others. Jesus invested His life in meeting the
    needs of others, and so should we. How can we say we follow
    Jesus and continue to live only for ourselves? Serving puts
    you in situations that will stretch you, grow you, and require
    additional faith. Serving others will require greater spiritual
    stamina than you've ever experienced. Yes, it can be exhausting,
    but this is how stamina is developed. Don't avoid it but instead
    embrace it.

If you want to have your faith strong, then you will need to do more than take a class and attend church. These might be great starting points, but they are no substitutes for the true spiritual workouts we all need to grow our faith. Is your faith getting stronger, or is it in the stages of atrophy? No matter where it is, exercise is the answer.

Scripture for the Day:

Hebrews 11

Thought for the Day:

What can you do to work out your faith? Think back through the three suggestions for growing your faith and ask yourself whether you do these steps. Which ones can you grow in?

GOOD RESULTS DON'T COME EASY

My alarm goes off at five-clock in the morning during my workweek. I roll out of bed instantly so I won't give myself the opportunity to rethink this decision. I'm not even remotely awake yet as I stumble into the bathroom and begin putting my gym clothes on. I grab my gym bag and sleepwalk into the kitchen, where my best friend in all the world is waiting for me … coffee. I pour the glorious nectar into my travel mug and head out the door. As I drive the four-mile trip to the gym, I drink as much of the scalding-hot, heavenly drink as my mouth can endure. Once at my destination, my early-morning workout begins. What do I do with my coffee? Pour it out? Not on your life! I drink it throughout my workout. I know you may think I'm crazy. My wife says I'm crazy. I do know this: if I want good results, they won't come easy. There is no easy way to be over fifty years old and be in shape. If I want certain results, I must be willing to pay for them.

Following Jesus is no different. We live in a culture where people want everything easy. We live in a culture obsessed with convenience. Every new gadget, every new advancement in technology, comes with the promise of making our lives more comfortable. We have come to expect, even demand, convenience and comfort. The problem is that we have also adopted this view of following Jesus. Sure, we want to follow as long as it doesn't get too uncomfortable. Surely Jesus wouldn't inconvenience my plans or schedule. This results in an anemic version of Christianity, where people don't experience the results they read about in the word of God. It would be like me complaining about not seeing any physical results as I lie in bed and ignore my alarm. If I want the results, they aren't acquired through comfort. If we desire the incredible results of following Jesus, they don't come easily either. First Timothy 4:7–8 says, "Train yourself to be godly. For physical training is of some value, but godliness has value for all things, holding promise for both the present life and the life to come."

Train yourself to be godly? Train? Yes, this is what it says. Are you in spiritual training, or are you AWOL? Are you lying in your spiritual bed, complaining about your lack of spiritual growth? Are you wondering why you have no spiritual muscle? Are you frustrated that your faith is so weak? Are you discouraged over the lack of spiritual joy and passion you experience? These things don't grow by osmosis. They must be worked out. The hard work of spiritual training must become a lifestyle. It must be something every one of us resolves to do. The results of following Jesus, which we desire, simply don't come easily. So how do we work out? Here are a few questions to consider.

- Do you work out with the word of God every day?
- Do you work out in prayer every day?
- Are you letting these workout times grow?
- Do you work out by serving the needs of others?
- Do you work out by being financially generous?
- Do you work out by being gracious, loving, and forgiving in your relationships?
- Do you work out by altering your time and schedule to prioritize these things?

Training is hard work, but the results of training are worth the effort. Following Jesus is an amazing journey, but it's not an easy one. It's not one that will be defined by comfort and convenience. It is a journey, though, that can be defined by fulfillment and joy. The writer of 1 Timothy said that training for "godliness has value for all things, holding promise for both the present life and the life to come." He's telling us it's worth it.

You want your faith to come alive? You want to experience God like never before? You want Him to use you to make a difference in this life? Would you like to see the word of God come alive in your own circumstances? Then hear the call of your Shepherd as He is asking you to follow Him. Roll out of the spiritual bed and out of the spiritual slumber you have been in. Get dressed for a workout. Pour yourself some glorious heavenly nectar and take the plunge. Say good-bye to comfort and to convenience being your greatest motivators. Say hello to the good results of a faith that is worked out by following Jesus. Easy? No way! Worth it? Oh yeah!

Scripture for the Day:

1 Corinthians 9:26–27

Thought for the Day:

What specific things can you do to work out your faith? What new spiritual habits need to be developed in your life? How does your current workout need to grow?

OVERCOMING EVIL

We live in a broken world. Terrorism, wars, famine, poverty, violence, and political unrest demand much of the attention from the media. As you watch the news, it's easy to feel hopelessness well up in your soul. There just seems to be such an overwhelming flood of evil that permeates this world. Sometimes I think the enormity of the whole thing can make us feel paralyzed. "Lord, what possibly can I do to battle against such overwhelming evil?" Believe it or not, God has an answer for you. Romans 12:21 says, "Do not be overcome by evil, but overcome evil with good."

Sounds too simple, doesn't it? Yet this is God's answer to us who live in a broken, fallen, evil-stained world. Battle the evil you see with good. For many, the evil seems so unconquerable that they do nothing. This is exactly what evil wants from us. Stay paralyzed and do nothing. We forget that evil isn't all powerful. We serve an all-powerful, ever-present, eternal, *good* God. Good has more power than evil. Do you believe this? Have you lost your faith in good? Have you lost your courage that one act of goodness can make a difference in this life? If you have, then evil is overcoming you. There's a solution. Do good!

I see many followers of Jesus who have allowed the rampant evil to cause them to become cynical. They no longer believe they can make a difference. They no longer believe the tide of evil can be stopped. They just hang on until death or until Jesus returns. Hardly "more than conquerors" like we are called in scripture, don't you think? We have forgotten that good is kryptonite to evil. Good is the antidote. Good is still the answer. Good still makes a difference.

As a pastor for over thirty years, I have seen how good makes a difference in the flood of evil. I have seen people giving up a night a week to serve a free dinner to homeless. I see others who sacrificed vacations to go to Guatemala and help children get out of poverty, have an education, and receive nutritious food. I see others who serve weekly at our resource center, providing food boxes and clothing to needy people. I see partnerships with city and county agencies as we work together, meeting needs. I listen to people as they refuse to give in to the verbal hopelessness and speak good words about a community they live in. I see others who purchase extra groceries so they can partner with local schools, providing weekend meals for close to two hundred children a week. I have the great privilege to work with a congregation of people who believe we overcome evil with good. I have a front-row seat and watch Romans 12:21 happen in our community.

What about you? As a follower of Jesus, you are called to overcome evil with good. Your one act of kindness and your generosity, service, and goodness matter. The power to turn back evil is in you because God lives in you. Your actions can now be an extension of His goodness in you. Your words even carry with them tremendous power. Refuse to speak and give a platform to the despair. Speak words of faith, truth, promise, and hope. Watch what happens. Evil gets turned back. People begin to have hope. Surely there will be some who think you're crazy. They'll look at you as just another unrealistic dreamer. Don't be discouraged. Be committed to a lifestyle of demonstrating God's goodness in an evil world.

Now, can you imagine what ten people could do? How about one hundred people? Maybe even one thousand people? The power of good can become exponential. Every move of God begins with one person who is reckless enough to believe God and follow Him. Will you be that one person? The evil in front of you has an enemy it cannot overcome. It's called "good," and that goodness is in your power to wield.

Scripture for the Day:

Romans 8:31–39

Thought for the Day:

Have you been allowing evil to win? Have you been losing hope that any difference can be made in this world? What good thing can you begin doing to make a difference in someone's life? What need can you begin meeting? Now go do it; and while you're at it, take someone else with you.

CONSISTENCY MAKES THE DIFFERENCE

Up in the hills above Molalla Oregon, there is a place called the Molalla River Corridor. Beyond Glen Avon Bridge, there is a stunning beauty of twelve miles of paved road following the Molalla River as it winds its way through the foothills of the Cascades, making its journey down to the valley below and to the town that carries its name. It is truly a remarkable and beautiful place. I have had the privilege of exploring this area all my life. There is a specific area most locals simply call "the narrows." It is where the river narrows to no more than ten to fifteen feet wide and has cut a deep narrow swath right through the basalt rock.

This deep-green, narrow passage is not only a unique and beautiful place; it is also a living example of consistency. This path wasn't made overnight. The relentless force of the water, multiplied over many years, has worn away even the hardest of surfaces. Its never-ending assault on the rock carved out this unusual yet picturesque spot. In fact, it continues to carve this path deeper today. It wasn't just the force of the water that created this wonder; it was the consistency that has made the difference over time.

For those of us who want to see change in our own lives, marriages, families, and communities, we must embrace the same mind-set. We must remain consistent, doing the right things over and over again often for years before we begin to see real, lasting change. Sometimes those old behaviors seem just as stubborn as the basalt rock. Sometimes our old way of doing things or relating to others is as hard as stone. Maybe even the environment of an entire community just seems to never change for the better. Yet our relentless pursuit of what is right, healthy, and pleases God isn't worthless. Consistently doing the right thing over time will eventually make a difference. Our commitment must be to never stop the flow of what is right, never stop the current of obedience. Even little acts of goodness often done over many years can make a difference. Hebrews 10:35–36 says, "So do not throw away your confidence; it will be richly rewarded. You need to persevere so that when you have done the will of God, you will receive what he has promised."

Here at Foothills we believe obedience to the word of God equals blessing. If we patiently endure doing what God wants, there is reward for this type of consistency. Often, though, people throw away this confident trust in the Lord and stop doing what He desires. They stop the flow of what is good and allow the hardness of this life to win and define their reality. But if water can erode rock, then our patient endurance in obedience can erode darkness. God's will, done repeatedly over a significant period of time, can change a life, a marriage, a family, and even a city. Yes, consistency in obedience matters.

Often, though, we desire quick fixes and instant gratification. This mentality sets us up for disappointment and failure. We want results now, and when we don't see them, we conclude that our efforts have no impact. We must remember the river. It is the constant flow of our relentless obedience that makes lasting change a reality. Change is difficult. Whether it's change in your own life, your marriage, or a community, the old ingrained thinking, attitudes, and behaviors are as resistant as rock. They change only with time. They yield only when we refuse to quit. Progress can be measured not in hours or days but in years and decades.

We must make the decision not to give up and give in to despair. What seems unchangeable can change when enough people decide to simply endure what is right. We must not expect quick fixes or superficial answers. We must embrace a relentlessness in our commitment to follow Jesus and practically live out His will. Therefore, don't quit following Jesus in your marriage. Don't give up on being a godly model to your kids. Don't stop loving people who refuse to accept your love. Don't give up on your community, no matter how broken it appears. Don't lose hope that your efforts matter. Consistency makes a difference. God says so! If you will stay the course, "...you will receive what he has promised." (Heb. 10:36). What has God promised? God has promised us so much more than this book has room to describe. Briefly, though, the promise is that obedience results in blessing— blessing in your life personally, in your marriage, in your relationships, and in ways that are beyond what you can ask or even imagine. Now isn't that worth being consistent for?

May God give you the desire and strength to be consistent in following Him. Whatever hard thing you're facing, keep in mind that it will eventually fall to the current of your relentless obedience. Stay the course, my friend. Remember the river.

Scripture for the Day:

2 Corinthians 4:8–18

Thought for the Day:

Where have you lost your confidence that obedience matters? Where do you need to keep the current of obedience flowing like a relentless river?

ARE YOU HEARING GOD?

One of the most precious experiences I get to have in this life is the personal communication of the God of the universe with me. My prayers aren't simply an endless monologue I commit to day after day for decades. Prayer is actually an ongoing dialogue with the God who loves me and sent His Son to die for me. Yes, God speaks. I know some people get a bit uncomfortable when I say things like, "Really, God talks to you." They ask this with a very puzzled look on their faces. Many think the idea that God speaks to us in this life is just a bit weird. What I think is odd is how many people who say they are followers of Jesus think prayer is a monologue. Many simply believe prayer and communication with God are only one way. Read the following scripture and think again about whether our relationship with Jesus is a monologue or dialogue.

> My sheep listen to my voice; I know them, and they follow me. (John 10:27)

> But when he, the Spirit of truth, comes, he will guide you into all the truth. He will not speak on his own; he will speak only what he hears, and he will tell you what is yet to come. (John 16:13)

> The Spirit told Philip, "Go to that chariot and stay near it." (Acts 8:29)

I could list hundreds of verses from the word of God that illustrate the fact that God is continually communicating with His people. This is seen in the Old Testament. It is seen in the New Testament. It is seen in Jesus' life. It is seen in the early church. Jesus leads and talks to His people. This is the normal experience of those who follow Him. It leaves me very puzzled when I see those who believe God would require us to communicate with Him in our prayers throughout our entire life but believe He will never say anything back. C'mon, think about this! That's just weird. What kind of a God do you think He is? How can you say you have a "personal relationship" with God if He never talks to you? Can you have a personal relationship with anyone else who never talks to you? Of course not! Relationships don't work this way. If someone never talks to you, the relationship isn't very personal. In fact, where is the relationship at all?

I have followed Jesus my entire adult life. Yes, God talks with me. God communicates with me. God gives me personal information regarding His will, plans, and desires for my life. "My sheep listen to my voice." (John 10:27). This is real, folks! Wouldn't you like to hear His voice too? Wouldn't you like the voice of your Shepherd to lead you? Wouldn't you like to go from the monologue to a living dialogue?

The skeptics often say, "Well, *how* is He going to speak to me? Am I supposed to hear some voice from heaven or something?" Don't get hung up with the method God may use. God can speak to you and me any way He wants. He's God! He's not limited in the ways He can communicate His heart to you. I have had Him speak to me through His word in life-changing ways as I sought His will and direction for my life. I have had His presence literally overwhelm me at times. I have had such strong inner promptings to do things that they were almost irresistible. I have heard God's voice through other godly people speaking into my life. I have experienced Him communicating to me His pleasure, love, and approval for this broken, flawed person I am. I have never heard an audible voice, but I have talked to plenty of people who have. God communicates to us in the way we need it. He talks with us in the way we recognize that it is Him, and it is tailor made for us. That is what makes it so precious. The method was designed just for you. You see, He knows how to speak your language. Remember, He made your heart; therefore, He knows how to communicate to you in the way your heart needs it.

So how do you take your praying from a boring, monotonous monologue to a dynamic dialogue? Here you go.

1. Ask God to speak to you. Ask Him to communicate with you. This is a faith step. If you don't believe He talks back, you will probably never ask Him to. Why not pray, "Lord, I truly want to hear Your voice so I can know You and follow You better"? That will put a smile on His face for sure.

2. Pray that God would improve your hearing and seeing. Jesus often talked about people having eyes and not seeing, and ears and not hearing. We need the veil lifted from our spiritual hearing and seeing.

3. Make sure your heart is right. Are you walking in obedience? Is sin confessed? Are your relationships right? Is there unforgiveness, bitterness, or gossip? All these things hinder our hearing. The channel through which God speaks needs to be unhindered. Remove the barriers, and you might be amazed by what you begin hearing.

Don't settle for a monologue any longer. The God who created and loves you is speaking. Let's have ears to hear.

Scripture for the Day:

Ephesians 6:18; Colossians 4:2; 1 Thessalonians 5:6

Thought for the Day:

As you pray, pay attention to those inner promptings you may have ignored in the past. Develop your alertness to His voice as He speaks to you.

CHAPTER 4

FOLLOWING JESUS WITH KINGDOM QUALITIES

LOVE: THE DEFINING QUALITY OF MY LIFE

If your spouse or close friend was asked to pick the top-three words that best describe your life, do you ever wonder what he or she would say? Would the friend use words like *loyal, carefree, fun, hardworking, patient, driven, spontaneous,* or possibly a multitude of others? Would he or she use the word *love*? Would you use this word to describe yourself? There are many words we could use to describe a follower of Jesus, but one word needs to be at the top of our list and aspirations. It's the word *love*. Love isn't a gender-specific word. It's not a word that describes women better than men. Love is specific to following Jesus. If there is one word that should best describe Jesus' followers, it is the word *love*.

Mark 12:28–31 says, "One of the teachers of the law came and heard them debating. Noticing that Jesus had given them a good answer, he asked him, 'Of all the commandments, which is the most important?' 'The most important one,' answered Jesus, 'is this: "Hear, O Israel: The Lord our God, the Lord is one. Love the Lord your God with all your heart and with all your soul and with all your mind and with all your strength." The second is this: "Love your neighbor as yourself." There is no commandment greater than these.'"

Just stop for a moment and consider how intense this command really is. We're not supposed to love God just a little bit; we don't add God to our list of affections. That's like saying I love to fish or shop or eat chocolate, and God is all in the same sentence. We're not asked to fit Him in to our list of loves. He wants to be our first love. But what does all this mean? Let's take the next few days to better understand how love is to be the defining quality of our lives.

It's significant to see that in Mark 12:30, the word *all* is mentioned four times, describing our love for God. What does this mean? Let's take one at a time. Today we'll look at what it means to love God with all your heart. The Bible describes the heart as the decision and control center of a person's being. To love God with all your heart means He is your first decision. He is the primary controller of your life. He is your number-one affection. Whoever or whatever controls your heart controls your life.

To love God with all your heart means you have settled the control issue of your life. Who is in charge? Who is calling the shots? Who gets to lead, and who gets to follow? Until this issue is settled, the other three areas fall apart. Until God has your heart, decisions, affections, and will, you will forever be a person with divided loyalties. Loving God with all your heart is more of a choice of the will rather than a feeling. The simple truth is that whoever controls your heart controls you.

Scripture for the Day:

John 21:12–17

Thought for the Day:

What affections control and consume your heart? Can you identify your greatest one? If Jesus asked you whether you love Him more than "these," how would you answer?

LOVING GOD WITH ALL YOUR MIND

There is a simple and effective activity every married couple can do to help their spouse feel loved. What is it? Tell him or her you were thinking about him or her. Sometimes it's just that simple. Maybe during the course of your crazy, chaotic day you simply took a few moments and shot off a text to your spouse, saying, "Hey, just wanted you to know I was thinking of you." Most people I know will feel loved by this type of outreach. Why? Because, if you're on someone's mind during his or her busy day, you must be quite the priority to him or her. Thinking about someone is connecting to *love*. Now let's apply this to loving God.

Remember, Jesus said to love God with all our minds (Mark 12:30). What does it mean to love God with all our minds? How does someone love with his or her mind? How do we do this? First, let's look at the issue of frequency. How often during a typical day do we think about our relationship with God? It's easy to simply and mentally disengage with God during the day or week. How are we loving God with our minds if we rarely think about our relationship with Him over the course of our day? Is there any surprise that we have no spiritual passion on Sunday at church when we rarely thought about God during the week? Thinking about someone is connecting to love.

Second, there is the issue of content. How much time during the day do we think about things we shouldn't? How often do we entertain materialistic thoughts, angry thoughts, and thoughts of unforgiveness? How often do our thoughts digress, becoming consumed with bitterness and revenge, not to mention fear and anxiety? Let's not forget the time spent in lust, selfishness, and pride. I think you get the picture. It's easy to have the entire day filled with this type of thinking. Loving God with all our minds isn't so easy.

Loving God with all our minds means we are going to give intentional attention to letting God transform our lives by transforming the way we think in frequency and content. Romans 12:2 talks about being "transformed by the renewing of our minds." I think this is one of the reasons we don't hear God much. We're not loving God with our minds. So often our minds are spiritually disengaged or in the wrong place.

By far one of the best ways to begin shaping your thoughts in a way that reflects a love for God is by developing the habit of reading God's word every day. If you have yet to grow this habit in your life, now would be the perfect time. God's word will help shape your thinking and also give you substitute thoughts for the ones you're trying to avoid. Prayer is such a practical way to tell God during the day, "Just wanted You to know I was thinking of You."

Scripture for the Day:

Romans 12:1–2

Thought for the Day:

What practical steps can you take to remind yourself of your relationship with God throughout the day so you can grow in loving Him with all your mind?

LOVING GOD WITH ALL YOUR STRENGTH

It takes energy to love someone. Love isn't simply a warm sentiment about a person. Love isn't only an emotional response. Love isn't merely nice thoughts. True love requires an investment of energy. It takes energy to love my wife. Even after twenty-eight years of marriage, I continue to invest the energy required so she feels loved. Real love does something; it takes action. Sometimes love requires that I wash the dishes, clean the bathroom, cook the dinner, or make her hot chocolate in the mornings. Sometimes love requires a tremendous amount of inner strength to love her cat as it sits in my gym bag, depositing hair everywhere. It takes strength to do the loving thing, even when you don't feel like it. Yes, love requires energy. I'm sure this is why the last way we are to love God is with our strength.

Remember, Jesus said we are to love God with all our strength (Mark 12:30).

What does it mean to love God with all my strength? If we love God with our hearts, souls, and minds, then it only makes sense that our love for God is reflected in our physical strength. We love God, even with our physical energy. How do we love God this way? Just think about our daily activities. It takes physical energy to serve God. It takes energy to go on mission trips and love others, energy God can use to make a difference in this life. It even takes physical energy to pray, to read my Bible, and even to worship. Love requires energy and strength.

Do we love God from our physical energy and strength, or do we give our best energy to the world? Are we always too tired to love people, to serve the needs of others, and to use the gifts and abilities God gave us for His glory? Are we too exhausted to get involved, too tired to care, or too drained to be burdened? To love God isn't an intellectual exercise. It isn't simply a mental agreement. It certainly has to be more than lip service. Loving God requires physical, mental, and even emotional strength.

Can you love God with your strength? This isn't about being strong; it's about giving God the strength you do have. It's not about preserving or protecting your energy; it's about loving God so much that you invest it and at times exhaust it in serving Him. Many people say they love God with their words. God is calling us to demonstrate that we love Him with our strength.

Scripture for the Day:

2 Corinthians 4:7–18

Thought for the Day:

How can you love God with your physical strength? Have you been avoiding service opportunities simply because they take too much energy? What physical thing can you do today to show God you love Him? Maybe it's time to look at your priorities. Do you have energy drainers in your life that are keeping you from loving God?

LOVING YOUR NEIGHBOR

Everyone has an annoying neighbor story. We lived next door to some neighbors who certainly tested our patience and love. They began the relationship with us by running over our flowers as they moved in. They were up at all hours of the night, running power equipment. Their friends would come over to their house and flick cigarette butts into our yard. I built a fence to help protect some privacy, only to have them accidently back into parts of it, breaking a few boards. Therefore, when Jesus says to love your neighbor as yourself, I cringe a little. Sometimes this is a tough one. Mark 12:31 says, "The second is this: 'Love your neighbor as yourself.' There is no commandment greater than these."

Who is my neighbor anyway? A neighbor is any needy person we come in contact with. When Jesus spoke of this command, someone was quick to ask Jesus who His neighbor was. I think that would have been me for sure. "Jesus, can I have some clarification please?" Jesus told a story or parable to illustrate and teach us who our neighbors are. They aren't just the people we live next door to. Jesus told a story most people refer to as the parable of the Good Samaritan in Luke 10:30–37. From the story, we discover that a neighbor is the following:

- Anyone whose needs I am aware of
- Anyone I encounter as I go about my daily life (He wasn't looking.)
- Anyone I encounter who can't help himself or herself
- Anyone other people have ignored and avoided (the rejects)

The standard for this type of love is how you love yourself. To love your neighbor as yourself is to demonstrate the same level of care, concern, and responsibility you would apply to yourself. If the injured man could have done these things, he would have. But he needed someone else to do it. Notice all the specific loving things the Samaritan did:

- He saw the man and felt compassion. (He didn't protect his heart.)
- He stopped to see and altered his agenda. (He didn't decide he was too busy.)
- He got personally involved by bandaging the wounds. (He got his hands dirty.)
- He was personally inconvenienced by putting the man on his own animal.
- He was financially committed by paying for the inn where he took the man to recover. (He didn't decide he didn't have enough to share.)
- He demonstrated genuine concern and responsibility because he told the innkeeper he would be back to check on him and pay more if necessary.

We are surrounded by people who desperately need to be loved. Their wounds may not be visible physically, but they are wounded deeply nonetheless. People walk right by them and ignore them every day. The abused, the broken, the lonely, the discouraged, and the depressed are all around us. You may be the only person to show them the love of God and let them know they matter. They may be a coworker, the girl who makes your coffee at Starbucks, the person across the aisle at church, and yes, maybe even your physical neighbor. One thing is for sure: they all need to know God loves them, and you may be their only chance to see it in action. Now what can you do to love them?

Scripture for the Day:

Luke 10:30–37

Thought for the Day:

Ask God to put one person on your mind to demonstrate love to today.

LOVING PEOPLE LIKE JESUS DOES

Loving people who are in need is just easy to wrap my mind and heart around. The Good Samaritan story just makes sense to me. But what about everyone else? What about all those people I go to church with? They're not helpless. They don't appear to be in some dire situation. In fact, they look pretty "put together" from where I sit. They have nice cars, houses, and clothes. Can't I just go to church and ignore everyone else? Some of these people I don't particularly care about anyway. It's not that they've done anything very bad to me; they just haven't done anything nice either. You know, it's easy to feel this way about others we may go to church with, yet Jesus asks us to love at an amazing level.

John 13:34–35 says, "A new command I give you: Love one another. As I have loved you, so you must love one another. By this everyone will know that you are my disciples, if you love one another."

We must love fellow believers as Jesus loves them. How does Jesus love us?

1. Jesus loves us unconditionally.
2. Jesus loves us sacrificially—He died for us!
3. Jesus loves us consistently. (He doesn't love *some* people or groups more than others; He doesn't love Baptists, Methodists, Nazarenes, or Foothills believers more.)
4. Jesus loves us by always forgiving us.
5. Jesus loves us by providing for us (physically, spiritually, emotionally, and relationally).

Do we love other believers like this? The standard for how we love one another is how Jesus loves us. That's a high standard. That's a crazy kind of love. I believe one of the primary places Satan attacks churches is in their commitment to love each other. If he can get followers of

Jesus fighting each other, holding grudges, harboring bitterness, or trying to manipulate one another, the church is no different from the world. Jesus didn't command us to just get along, just tolerate each other, or simply put up with one another. No! He told us to love each other like He loves us. Why? Because this is a direct result of obeying this command.

We must love fellow believers to prove to the world that Jesus is real. It isn't our convincing arguments that will prove to the world that Jesus is real. It won't be our programs, ministries, beautiful buildings, or any class we offer. What will prove to the world that Jesus is real are the relationships we experience. One of the greatest heresies of the modern church isn't doctrinal heresy but a relational heresy that believes we can effectively follow Jesus without loving one another radically like Jesus said. The Bible teaches no such thing. To follow Jesus is to commit to love like Jesus loves.

Scripture for the Day:

1 John 4:7–21

Thought for the Day:

What does it look like to grow in your commitment to love your fellow followers of Christ? How can you demonstrate love toward them just like Jesus has shown love for you?

FORGIVENESS

Let's face it; some of the things Jesus asks us to do are tough. One of the most difficult yet liberating choices we can make in response to others is to forgive them. Now, I realize most people agree that this is a good thing to do, but it's certainly not easy. I've had people lie about me, gossip about me, create false rumors, post nasty stuff on Facebook, and try to destroy my good reputation, which took me a lifetime to build. This is the short list, of course, but I bet most of you reading this can relate. Some of you have experienced much worse than what I described. You carry deep wounds from those who have caused you inexcusable pain. "Forgiveness?" you say. I know … this is a tough topic.

Simply put, forgiveness is releasing others of any debt they may owe us. When people wound us, they now "owe us." They have created an emotional debt that, in our sense of fairness, needs to be repaid somehow. The problem is that there is no way they can ever repay or make up for what they have done. The wound is there. The pain was felt. Brokenness now remains. The solution Jesus described seems crazy. It is the exact opposite of what our emotions want and demand. Yet this irrational step of forgiveness is the only action that will set us free. To not forgive our offenders is to forever be their emotional prisoner. It is to forever be controlled by those who wounded us. It is to give up emotional control to someone else. I know it sounds hard, maybe even impossible, but listen to the word of God once again on this topic.

Then Peter came to Jesus and asked, "Lord, how many times shall I forgive my brother or sister who sins against me? Up to seven times?" Jesus answered, "I tell you, not seven times, but seventy-seven times." (Matt. 18:21–22)

> Bear with each other and forgive one another if any of
> you has a grievance against someone. Forgive as the
> Lord forgave you. (Col. 3:13)

My guess is, you probably have someone you need to forgive today. Why would I say this? Because relational pain is one of the common threads of humanity. Because you exist, I know you have been wounded. We live in a broken world among broken people. Therefore, if we don't learn to forgive, we lose more and more emotional freedom with each passing day. How about trusting Jesus with your emotions? Today could be that first step toward forgiveness. I say "first step" because the reality of forgiveness is that it is a process. But every process begins with a choice. Why not take that first step now and trust Jesus with the rest of the process? Your freedom awaits!

Scripture for the Day:

Mark 11:25; Ephesians 4:32

Thought for the Day:

Our standard for forgiving others is to be understood in light of how God has forgiven us. Spend some time today thinking of, and thanking God for, how profound His forgiveness of you is.

TRUTH AND GRACE

As Jesus was teaching in the temple, there was again a large crowd hanging on His every word. Suddenly, there was a loud commotion toward the back. There was yelling and screaming, and soon the crowd began to part as men shouted, "Let us through!" Shortly they made their way to the front to Jesus. The religious leaders brought a woman, who was mortified, embarrassed, and shamed in front of this crowd of strangers. They told Jesus she had been caught in the very act of adultery. They threw her down in front of Jesus and the astonished audience. The religious leaders quoted the law of Moses, which gave them permission to stone such a person guilty of such an action. They demanded to know what Jesus thought should be done.

Jesus simply bent down and wrote in the dust. They pressed Jesus further, demanding an answer. Finally, Jesus stood up and said, "You who are without sin throw the first stone." Read what happened next. "At this, those who heard began to go away one at a time, the older ones first, until only Jesus was left, with the woman still standing there. Jesus straightened up and asked her, 'Woman, where are they? Has no one condemned you?' 'No one, sir,' she said. 'Then neither do I condemn you,' Jesus declared. 'Go now and leave your life of sin'" (John 8:9–11).

Jesus modeled something that is often in short supply among His followers today: the combination of truth and grace. In this scene, we see that Jesus addressed this woman with both. After all her accusers are gone, Jesus told her He didn't condemn her for her actions. That's grace! Too often people stop reading right at this point, or maybe they simply quit paying attention. Jesus went on to say, though, "Go and sin no more." In other words, "Adultery is a sin; now you need to stop doing this." That's truth! Too often we simply see Jesus as the Champion who doesn't condemn the sinner, but that is only half the story. Jesus is the One who doesn't condemn the sinner so He can provide the truth that sets the sinner free.

What changes our lives is the combination of grace and truth. Grace without truth promotes the idea that our behavior doesn't matter. Jesus just loves us anyway, no matter what. It's true that my behavior doesn't alter God's love for me, but thinking that my actions don't matter to Him is completely and biblically wrong. Jesus wants to transform the people He loves. Therefore, in this environment of love, grace, and acceptance, He gives us His truth that can set us free from sin. Our sin matters. Sin is still a big deal to Jesus. It was our sin that sent Him to the cross. Without truth, our lives don't change. Without truth, we look, act, and behave just like this world. Christianity can't simply be only grace.

Truth, though, must be given in the environment of grace. Without grace truth can be cold, harsh, condemning, and judgmental. Truth without this gracious environment makes people feel judged and hopeless. Truth without grace makes people feel crushed under the weight of their sin, and they struggle rather than find inspiration to change. Truth sets us free as we experience it in the right environment. Unfortunately, many followers of Jesus have used truth to wound people instead of heal them. The very gift that should have brought hope to people brought condemnation because it was shared in the wrong environment.

If we want to be like Jesus, we must be people who are all-grace and all-truth type of people. It's not one or the other; it's both. The world needs to see this balance in Jesus' followers. We must passionately and profoundly love all people regardless of their sin and lifestyle choices, past or present. We must also never be ashamed of the truth of the word of God. Truth doesn't condemn when it is experienced in the environment of love and grace. Truth doesn't change simply because it is no longer politically correct. If we believe truth sets people free

(John 8:32), then to remove truth is to remove the power of the gospel. If we remove grace, we've removed the main reason why people want to hear truth.

Let's be more like Jesus in this world.

"Jesus straightened up and asked her, 'Woman, where are they? Has no one condemned you?' 'No one, sir,' she said. 'Then neither do I condemn you,' Jesus declared. 'Go now and leave your life of sin.'" (John 8:11)

Scripture for the Day:

Galatians 6:1–3

Thought for the Day:

Which one do you need to work on to act more like Jesus—grace or truth? Who are the people to whom you need to demonstrate grace and truth?

WE'RE BETTER TOGETHER

We have become a culture obsessed with the rights of the individual. Now don't get me wrong; I'm glad we have a society and a Constitution that clarifies these rights. The dilemma is that we have become hyper committed to the individual and have lost our perspective of the whole. Society tells us that the individual is always more important than the whole. When John F. Kennedy gave his inaugural address on January 20, 1961, he made a famous statement: "Ask not what your country can do for you—ask what you can do for your country." This phrase wouldn't even make sense in our culture today. It seems we are moving more and more in a direction where everyone is more concerned with what's in it for him or her as individuals.

Because this is the culture we, the followers of Jesus, are exposed to, it's easy for us to adopt this perspective spiritually. What's in it for me? What can Jesus do for me? How does Jesus bless me? Then we make the natural progression to the church. What can the church do for me? What does the church offer me? Often this concept is expressed as, "Ask not what you can do for your church; ask what your church can do for you." We completely lose the perspective that we, the church, are the body of Christ. We are a family. We are a collection of believers who make up a greater whole. It's not simply all about Jesus and *me*. The biblical reality is that life is about Jesus and *us*. We aren't better alone as individuals. We are better only as we live, walk, and serve together.

> Even so the body is not made up of one part but of many. Now if the foot should say, "Because I am not a hand, I do not belong to the body," it would not for that reason stop being part of the body. And if the ear should say, "Because I am not an eye, I do not belong to the body," it would not for that reason stop being part of the body. If the whole body were an eye, where

would the sense of hearing be? If the whole body were an ear, where would the sense of smell be? But in fact God has placed the parts in the body, every one of them, just as he wanted them to be. If they were all one part, where would the body be? As it is, there are many parts, but one body. The eye cannot say to the hand, "I don't need you!" And the head cannot say to the feet, "I don't need you!" (1 Cor. 12:14–21)

Are you following the imagery here? We collectively make up the body of Christ. An individual alone cannot represent the body of Christ. You and I are simply a piece of a greater whole. The only way we experience the greatest benefit from our relationship with Jesus is to give up our individualistic mind-set and embrace the fact that we need other believers in Christ. I cannot just be interested in getting my piece of the spiritual pie while I ignore others. It's not enough to simply be spiritually self-centered so that I care only about my spiritual needs and ignore the greater cause of Jesus' church. The power of the church happens only when we are together. The body functions only when all the parts are necessary. We will never do great things for the kingdom of God alone. We're better together.

Our obsession with ourselves and our spiritual "What's in it for me?" attitude is destroying the influence Jesus designed the church to have in this world. The transformational power of the church working together for a cause that is greater than any one person alone is being lost. We've traded a gospel that has transformational power to change nations for one designed to simply make us happy. We have become "American" followers of Jesus instead of followers of Jesus who happen to be American.

The hope for our future will never be in figuring out how to give people more rights. We have more rights than any other time in the history of the world. We are also the most unfulfilled. It seems that the pursuit of self just isn't working out too well. The hope for the future will be believers in Jesus showing their willingness to give up their rights to follow Him faithfully and serve together for a greater cause. Jesus said that if you want to save your life, you have to lose it. If you really want to follow Him, you must deny yourself. That's a very different message than the one of our culture, but I'm betting that what Jesus says is true. We're better together.

Scripture for the Day:

Luke 9:23–25

Thought for the Day:

Are you an American follower of Jesus or a follower of Jesus who happens to be American? How can you tell the difference?

MANAGING YOURSELF VS. MANAGING YOUR SCHEDULE

Years ago, I received some advice that has guided me for over twenty-five years. It came from an amazing man and teacher named Howard Hendricks. He said something like this: "It's always easier to manage a schedule than it is to manage yourself." Boy, have I found that to be true! What he was trying to communicate to us young students at the time was the need to discipline our lives. If you can train your schedule to reflect your values, you can train your life. Spend time deciding how your time reflects your goals and then create a schedule to reflect that. Stop trying to manage yourself. That's impossible. Our moods, desires, motivations, and emotions constantly change. Investing enormous amounts of energy trying to manage that will only be exhausting and discouraging. Instead, create a schedule that is highly personal to you and reflects who you want to be. Now submit your life to that schedule, regardless of how you feel. That advice has made a difference in my life for years.

I'm sure this is at least one reason why I became a very structured person. Years ago I created structure to help me live in the way I felt God was taking my life. I knew I could manage a schedule. Trying to manage myself was easily more than a handful. If the teachers, parents, and other leaders in my life couldn't manage me, who was I to think I could? I could, however, submit my life to a highly personalized schedule. I know some of you are already squirming as you read this, but is it any different from the exhortations we have from God's word? Look!

Train yourself to be godly. (1 Tim. 4:7)

Everyone who competes in the games goes into *strict training*. They do it to get a crown that will not last, but we do it to get a crown that will last forever. Therefore

> I do not run like someone running aimlessly; I do not fight like a boxer beating the air. No, *I strike a blow to my body and make it my slave* so that after I have preached to others, I myself will not be disqualified for the prize. (1 Cor. 9:25–27, emphasis added)

Brothers and sisters, I do not consider myself yet to have taken hold of it. But one thing I do: Forgetting what is behind and *straining toward what is ahead, I press on* toward the goal to win the prize for which God has called me heavenward in Christ Jesus. (Phil. 3:13–14, emphasis added)

All these verses imply tremendous intentionality. Whether it is "strict training," "making my body my slave," or "straining towards what is ahead," all require planning, scheduling, and determination to choose a particular type of lifestyle rather than allowing the demands of life to dictate our existence. Our lives are the sum of our choices. If you don't like your life, begin making different choices. I have chosen a highly personalized schedule that reflects my choices on what life I want to live. In fact, I cannot follow Jesus any other way. If I want to follow Him effectively in this life, I'm going to have to create a schedule that reflects that.

I hear people all the time: "I don't have time to come to church regularly." "I don't have time to serve." "I don't have time to get involved in that class or group." "I don't have time to go on that mission trip." "I don't have time to pray and read my Bible." My question to you is, why? Why are you allowing the demands of life to define what type of life you're living? Why are you allowing yourself to become a prisoner to a lifestyle you don't even enjoy? Do you really believe Jesus thinks it's acceptable to be so consumed by life's scattered demands that you can simply ignore the lifestyle He calls us to?

Folks, we get only one shot at this life. What life are you waiting for? Instead of waiting for it, why not decide to live it? Does your schedule reflect your values, goals, and lifestyle of following Jesus? Part of training ourselves to be godly is living a schedule that helps us do just that. Does yours? Maybe it's time to evaluate your schedule and make some changes. Remember, your schedule must be highly personalized to you. My schedule won't work for you. Do you really want to meet me at the gym at five o'clock in the morning? I didn't think so. Trust Jesus to show you where to begin making changes. Training and discipline don't take life away from you. Please don't believe this lie. Learning to discipline yourself through your schedule is what will give life to you. What life are you waiting for? First Timothy 4:7 says, "Train yourself to be godly."

Scripture for the Day:

Mark 1:29–39

Did Jesus' values determine His schedule?

Thought for the Day:

Are you *waiting* for another life, or are you *choosing* it? Are the chaotic demands around you driving your schedule? Or do you predetermine it? Does your schedule help you or hinder you from following Jesus?

HUMILITY: HOW GOD'S KINGDOM WORKS

I love to fish. Living in the Pacific Northwest allows us ample fishing opportunities with our vast networks of rivers, streams, and the coast less than two hours away. Since I love to fish so much, I also enjoy hanging out with other fishermen. They say that only 10 percent of fishermen catch 90 percent of the fish. In my experience, that is a pretty accurate statement. I catch my share of fish, but then there are those guys who are almost mysteriously good. They are people you love to hate—if you know what I mean. They always catch fish when no one else does. I purposely try to hang out with people like that. Why? They simply know how things work in the kingdom of fish that other people don't know. They understand subtle nuances that others miss. Every time I spend a day on the water with a person like that, I learn some new nugget of fishing truth that helps me put more fish in my boat.

Sometimes we can feel this way regarding our relationship with Jesus. Why do some people experience His presence, power, resources, and provision more consistently than others? Do only 10 percent of believers truly experience these things on a consistent basis, while others are left wanting? Though no one can answer such a question, I can tell you that more people should be experiencing these blessings. Why don't they? They simply don't understand how God's kingdom works. Because of their confusion, they don't catch the blessings from God that He desires them to have.

So here is a nugget of spiritual truth that could transform your experience with Jesus. His kingdom works off humility. The more you understand this fact, the more your experience of following Jesus will be transformed. Just read the following verses and see what humility brings:

You save the humble. (Ps. 18:27)

He guides the humble in what is right and teaches them his way. (Ps. 25:9)

The Lord sustains the humble. (Ps. 147:6)

God opposes the proud but shows favor to the humble. (James 4:6)

Humble yourselves before the Lord, and he will lift you up. (James 4:10)

God saves, guides, teaches, sustains, favors, and lifts up the humble. Humility unleashes the experiential presence of God and power of God in our lives. The more we resist, the more independently we behave; the more we demand that God operate by *our* understanding and time frames, the less of Jesus we will experience. I see believers constantly demanding that God give them life while they are unwilling to give up the very life that stands in the way of their request. In following Jesus, death precedes life. We must humble ourselves and give up this natural life for the life He wants to bring us. To live, you have to die first. This is what Jesus said. We must deny ourselves, take up our cross, and follow Jesus. That requires humility.

Whatever situation you find yourself in, the answer is to humble yourself before God. Are you discouraged? Are you struggling in your marriage? Did you lose your job? Do you have financial stress? Do you have an ongoing medical issue? Are you haunted by some issue from your past? Whatever the need may be, the first step is to humble yourself before God rather than to ask Him to change the situation. Humility unleashes God's resources.

What does this humility look like? It looks like Jesus in the garden of Gethsemane hours before His crucifixion. With the stress of the cross just moments away and while sweating drops of blood, Jesus told His Father, "Not my will but yours be done." (Luke 22:42). This is the true test of humility.

Are you willing to trust Jesus so much that you will walk a course you truly don't want to travel? Will you still humble yourself if He lets you lose your job? Can you tell God that you will trust Him, even if He allows the sickness to last? Will you trust Him regardless of the circumstances you are currently facing and say, "Lord, if this is a path You want me to walk, I trust You and submit my life to You"? This is what "death to self" looks like. But take heart because this is what unleashes the presence and power of God in your life. Why? Because this is how God's kingdom works.

Scripture for the Day:

Luke 9:23–26; 22:39–46

Thought for the Day:

Do you struggle with the concept of biblical humility? Is your life truly given up for God to do with it as He wishes? How much of your life are you still holding on to? Have you experienced what Jesus said—that in order to live you have to die first? How is Jesus calling you to embrace humility?

CHAPTER 5

EMPOWERED BY FOLLOWING JESUS

CONSISTENT GROWTH

I loved watching my kids grow. I truly appreciated each new season, discovery, and mark on the wall as we documented their physical progress. If there wasn't growth, something would have been drastically wrong. Not only did they physically grow, but they also grew mentally and emotionally. Their knowledge grew as they changed grades in school. Our conversations changed as they matured. It was all part of the natural process. Consistent growth is the norm.

Unfortunately, what is reality in the physical realm isn't always true spiritually. Though our children naturally grew up physically, we don't naturally grow up spiritually. Consistent spiritual growth must be a conscious effort. Make no mistake about it, though; it is God's heart for us to grow up. Ephesians 4:14–15 says, "Then we will no longer be infants, tossed back and forth by the waves, and blown here and there by every wind of teaching and by the cunning and craftiness of people in their deceitful scheming. Instead, speaking the truth in love, we will grow to become in every respect the mature body of him who is the head, that is, Christ."

Physical age and maturity have nothing to do with spiritual age and maturity. We all naturally get older physically, but we must be intentional to grow older spiritually. This growth isn't automatic. Notice in the scripture above that we shouldn't be like immature children. It's okay to start here but not okay to stay here. God wants us to consistently grow, but how are we to grow? Look back at Ephesians 4: "Grow to become in every respect the mature body of him who is the head, that is, Christ." In other words, our lives are to grow so that we continually look more and more like Jesus. Too many people are satisfied with being spiritual infants instead of pressing on to experience the richness of spiritual maturity.

Are you pressing on in your spiritual growth maturity, or have you stalled out? If you're ready to get moving again, let me give you some suggestions to get you heading in the right direction.

1. Desire spiritual growth. Let yourself be unsatisfied with your current maturity.
2. Pray for spiritual growth. Tell God you're serious about moving forward.
3. Be intentional with spiritual growth. This means being consistent with reading your Bible, taking notes during messages, taking classes offered at your church, and being more intentional at learning God's word.
4. Accept the discomfort of spiritual growth. Spiritual growth will require the application of God's truth to real-life situations. The applications can be uncomfortable, yet this step is required for genuine spiritual growth to take place. Without this step, growth is impossible.

Both of my daughters are now adults; they've married and have their own children. I wouldn't trade the richness of our current relationships for anything. I'm so glad they have grown up to be adult followers of Jesus who love their dad. What I would have missed out on if they'd never grown up to maturity. The blessings of adulthood have given me great sons-in-law and now grandchildren. These blessings are priceless and beyond words to describe. Spiritual adulthood likewise brings with it a host of blessings and a deep richness in our experience with Jesus that is worth all the effort it takes. Are you giving yourself to this journey?

Scripture for the Day:

1 Peter 2:2–3

Thought for the Day:

How would you describe your spiritual journey so far? Do you feel as if you've stalled out? Why? With God's help, what can you do to begin the journey of spiritual growth again?

DON'T EVER GIVE UP

Sometimes Jesus told some strange stories to illustrate a truth. In Luke 18, Jesus told a story about a poor widow and an unrighteous judge. The widow needed legal protection from someone, but the judge didn't care. She was persistent in going to the judge day after day. She was relentless in her requests and in her pursuit. Finally, exhausted after maybe days and possibly weeks, the unrighteous judge granted the widow her request before she completely wore the poor guy out. Can't you just see Jesus telling this story with a smirk on His face? This is the story He shared to help us understand prayer.

> Then Jesus told his disciples a parable to show them that they should always pray and not give up. (Luke 18:1)

> And the Lord said, "Listen to what the unjust judge says. And will not God bring about justice for his chosen ones, who cry out to him day and night? Will he keep putting them off?" (Luke 18:6–7)

I know I have been guilty of giving up. I know I have stopped praying. I have felt like God was "putting me off." Maybe I simply concluded that the answer was no, and it was time to just move on. I bet you have had experiences like this when it comes to prayer. You don't see any tangible answer after a while and start asking yourself, "What's the point?" Jesus' telling of this story answers this question. Apparently, there is a point. It seems that persistence in prayer has value in His eyes.

Why is persistence important? I will never be able to answer this question completely, but I do know several things. First, persistence keeps me connected to the only One who can change what I am requesting. Since prayer is primarily a relational experience, persistence keeps me connected relationally. Second, God allows our prayers to matter to Him and move Him to act. I like to think prayers carry spiritual weight in them. Some requests simply require more prayer to move because they are spiritually weighty issues. The more we pray, the more weight we put on the spiritual scales that will eventually reach a tipping point. Quit too soon, and the scales may never tip. We simply need to keep praying, knowing that our prayers matter to Him and that they are never meaningless in their spiritual significance.

If you have given up asking God for something or possibly someone, maybe it is time to pick up that torch again. Maybe you have been praying for years or even decades without a hint of answer. How do you know that the scales may be close to a tipping point? Now isn't the time to quit. Now is the time to pray and never give up.

Scripture for the Day:

Colossians 4:2

Thought for the Day:

How long should we pray? Something that has always helped me is PUSH: Pray Until Something Happens. Don't be afraid to PUSH. This isn't disrespectful before God. It is faith!

THE STRUGGLE

Let's just get this on the table: Following Jesus in this life is hard. In fact, following Jesus is the hardest thing I've ever tried to do in my entire life. Why do I say this? Because the struggle we experience never goes away. Of course there is peace, joy, His power, and the gratification of God's presence. Of course, we revel in the promises of God, but the sad reality is that this internal struggle with sin just never goes away in this life.

Sometimes I get tired of the battle. Sin just never takes a vacation. My fleshly desires don't take a holiday. I got saved, and Jesus put a new nature inside me, but my flesh didn't get saved. It's still as fallen as it ever was. There are days when I feel the struggle more than others. How about you? Here's how the apostle Paul described this struggle: "So I say, walk by the Spirit, and you will not gratify the desires of the flesh. For the flesh desires what is contrary to the Spirit, and the Spirit what is contrary to the flesh. They are in conflict with each other, so that you are not to do whatever you want" (Gal. 5:16–17)

I feel the opposition. There are days I get so discouraged because of this struggle. Don't you? Sometimes I feel like I should be beyond that struggle, that temptation, that wrong thought, yet there it is again, tormenting my soul. Now before we all get discouraged, notice the answer to this dilemma in verse 16. "Walk by the Spirit and you will not gratify the desire of the flesh." There is a solution. Dependency! That's learning to tap into His Spirit He put inside us so we can win this war. We haven't been left defenseless. His Spirit is in the battle with us.

If you're struggling with your own internal battles, let me encourage you. The battle that rages inside you is normal. No, nothing is wrong with you, but focusing on your struggle will never help you win. The focus is on His Spirit. It doesn't matter how many times today you have already blown it. Run back to Jesus and submit yourself once again to His Spirit's control. Don't allow your guilt to keep you from this process. The longer you delay running back to Him, the greater your struggle will become. God knows you struggle. He's not surprised by it. He's made a way for you to win this battle. His Spirit is in you. Now, seek His control over your life once again.

As long as we live in this broken world, we will continue the struggle with our fleshly desires. It's time to get up again. It's time to run back to Him again. It's time to make a commitment to never throw in the towel or surrender to your flesh. Power comes from surrendering to His Spirit in you. You can do this. Why? His Spirit is in you.

Scripture for the Day:

Romans 7:14–25; 8:1

Thought for the Day:

When you are in the midst of your struggle with your fleshly desires, do you obsess over the struggle, the sin, and your failure? Or do you run back to Jesus and submit to His Spirit? Which strategy do you think will result in victory?

PLUGGING INTO THE POWER

This life can certainly leave us feeling weak. This "weakness" we feel isn't always physical. Often it is much deeper than that. The weakness is internal, emotional, mental, and even spiritual fatigue. Sometimes we find ourselves spent. We have no more to give. The tank is on empty. In fact, maybe you feel like you're running in a deficit each day. You might even be wondering what's wrong with you. There's nothing wrong with you at all. You are experiencing what every human being on the planet faces at times. Our limited resources aren't enough for this life.

The good news is that we don't have to live merely on our resources. We can plug into and experience God's power in this life. There are so many promises about God's power being made available to His people in His word. Here are just a few to consider:

> But we have this treasure in jars of clay to show that this all-surpassing power is from God and not from us. (2 Cor. 4:7)

> For the Spirit God gave us does not make us timid, but gives us power, love and self-discipline. (2 Tim. 1:7)

> I can do all this through him who gives me strength. (Phil. 4:13)

The question is, why are so few people experiencing this power? If God has made His power available, where is it? Let me explain how God's power works.

For those of you who have accepted Jesus as your Lord and Savior, God's power is now in you. His power is in you because Jesus is in you. The potential to tap into God's unlimited resources are now made available to you. Notice a key word, though: *potential*. The potential to experience His power is in you. You and I must learn how to plug into this power. It's not automatic. It's not a guarantee. So how do we get it?

First, this power is a relational power. In John 15 Jesus said we must "abide" in Him. He went on to say in this passage that "without Me you can do nothing." Therefore, the first place to begin accessing this power is relationally. Are you relationally connected to Jesus? Is your heart right? Are you confessing your sin? Are you aware of the things in your life that hinder your intimacy with Jesus? Are you communicating with Him throughout the day? Is there a genuine relationship or simply a belief in Jesus? Remember, His power is relational power. It is accessed only through a relationship.

Second, His power is reserved for those who follow Him. God's power will never be given to those who want to live independently from Him and His ways. We must understand that power is reserved for obedience. Obedience triggers the power of God in our lives. God will never empower *your* thing. He only empowers *His* thing. This fact tends to be a hurdle for so many believers in Jesus. Just because they invited Jesus into their lives, they expect to access God's power, even though they don't follow Him daily. God will never empower you to live in a manner that is contrary to His word. Therefore, if you earnestly desire God's power in your life, the next step is to make a sincere commitment to obey what He says in His word.

You and I don't have to live our lives in a deficit. We don't have to feel overwhelmed constantly by life's pressures and demands. There is a power in us because Jesus is in us. In your hands you hold the plug of relationship and the plug of obedience. It's entirely up to you whether you plug into the source that's in you. The power is already hardwired in you. Isn't it time to plug in?

Scripture for the Day:

2 Corinthians 12:8–10

Thought for the Day:

What can you do today to connect relationally with Jesus? What is your level of commitment to obedience? Are there some changes that need to be made so you can experience the power of God that is already in you?

HAPPINESS

"I just want to be happy" is a phrase I have heard countless times over the years as I've listened to some desperate person sitting in my office or across the table at lunch. "Is this too much to ask?" is usually what I hear next. It's as if people want some reassurance that they aren't being unreasonable with the simple desire for happiness. It's almost like they are waiting for someone to give them justification for their discouragement. Many people do, in fact, justify this statement. "Yes, you deserve to be happy" is a statement I often hear in response. Although well intended, these types of comments only add to the emotional desperation and despair. They affirm the feelings yet provide no hope out of the dark predicament of the soul.

We set ourselves up for much of this because we believe happiness is just supposed to "happen" to us. Even phrases like "Happiness will find you" imply that happiness is floating around out there somewhere, and eventually it will discover you, land on you, or make its way into your life. This type of thinking is the fast track to being miserable. We set ourselves up for unhappiness by believing these myths. Experiencing happiness in this life doesn't really have to be so mysterious. Wanting to be happy isn't a bad desire. We simply need to go about it in the right way. Want to be happy? Here you go:

1. Happiness is a choice. That's right—happiness isn't floating around out there, waiting to find you. Happiness is the result of the choices you and I make. Most people simply make choices that result in being unhappy rather than happy. There is no escalator you can ride that will take you to the pinnacle of happiness. You must make choices. Remember, our lives are the sum of our choices, not the sum of our circumstances.

2. Choose God. Now, I realize most people don't equate happiness with God, but the Bible does. Our greatest source for happiness

in this world is our relationship with the living God. God can satisfy the desires of the human heart. Psalm 37:4 says, "Take delight in the Lord, and he will give you the desires of your heart." God knows your desires. He knows the deepest longings of your broken heart. He does care. He does see. Go to Him and give Him your unhappiness, despair, wounding, and longings. Give up on finding happiness your way and be broken enough to consider God's way. Before there is resurrection, there has to be death. Whatever it is you think you deserve, let it go ... Let it die at the feet of Jesus and wait.

3. Choose to serve others. The self-absorbed life is another great lie of our culture that is making people miserable at an alarming rate. The truth is, the more you obsess about yourself, the more unhappy you become. If you want to begin moving in the "happiness" direction, believe Jesus when He calls us to live our lives to serve others. As you get involved in the lives of other people, you will begin to feel something you haven't felt in a long time ... joy. Philippians 2:3–4 says, "Rather, in humility value others above yourselves, not looking to your own interests but each of you to the interests of the others."

4. Choose generosity. The opposite of this is another example of being self-absorbed. Once again, it has been proved over and over again by the experiences of countless people as well as by documented secular research; generous people are happier than stingy people. Generosity has nothing to do with income and everything to do with the heart. Our money and our hearts are connected. This is why the way you think and handle money impacts you emotionally. Want to be happier today? Pay for the coffee of the person behind you in line, perhaps the mom in the minivan going through the fast-food drive-through with screaming kids. Give the waitress a bigger tip than normal; take the clothes you never wear anymore to a homeless shelter. Just

try it and see. Matthew 6:21 says, "For where your treasure is, there your heart will be also."

5. Choose loving relationships. Loneliness and unhappiness go hand in hand. Since God created us as relational beings, we have an insatiable need to connect deeply and authentically with others. Relational isolation is another fast track to unhappiness. In our electronic age, where we spend more time looking at screens than we do at faces, it's no wonder loneliness is an epidemic. No screen will satisfy the need for face-to-face interaction. We must choose to engage. Choose to go to church. Choose to get involved in a small group of some kind. Serve alongside others in a project. Choose to forgive. Choose to give grace. Choose to recognize your desperate need for other imperfect people like you and put yourself in those environments. Yes, I know; this can be scary, but the result touches one of the deepest needs of your heart ... to be loved.

Scripture for the Day:

Deuteronomy 30:19–20

Thought for the Day:

What "happiness choices" can you begin to make instead of waiting for happiness to find you?

ARE YOU MALNOURISHED?

My wife and I recently entered a new season of our lives together, the season of being grandparents. Both of our daughters have been married for a few years, and both had their first child seven months apart from each other. Two grandchildren were born in a span of seven months—it can't get much better than that. Our first grandchild is a girl named Melody. Our second grandchild is a boy named Carter. Everyone kept telling us how amazing it was to be grandparents: how much fun it was, how different it was, and how unique it was compared to parenting. You know what? They were all right. It's better than anything I could have imagined. If you're a grandparent, you know what I'm talking about.

Watching them change is fascinating. When Lisa and I were having kids, I was finishing school, doing ministry full-time, and just trying to figure out life. I don't think I marveled at all about the growth that took place over the course of time. I'm making up for it now. One thing I've noticed is that food and growth go together. (I know that's rather obvious.) If there is one thing both my grandkids are good at it is letting everyone know when it's time to have food. These sweet, innocent, precious, angelic faces can turn into loud, obnoxious, demanding, unreasoning babies. It's food they crave, and you'd better get it to them in a hurry. When they finally get that bottle, they can devour it with a ferocity that is surprising. Get them fed, and the angels return, and the growth continues.

This is the imagery the Bible uses as it describes our process of spiritual growth. First Peter 2:2 says, "Like newborn babies, crave pure spiritual milk, so that by it you may grow up in your salvation."

The pure spiritual milk the author is referring to is the word of God, the Bible. I know, you may be thinking, *The Bible?* Yes. We need to crave a steady intake of God's word just as much as a baby craves that big bottle of milk. Most people I know look at the Bible more like eating broccoli or asparagus than something good. We read it because we have to. We read it because it's good for us. We certainly don't crave it or devour it with ferocity like a hungry baby. Yet this is the imagery we are given. This passage tells us that food and growth go together. I know, that's rather obvious … or is it?

We live in an age when we have more access to the word of God than at any time in the history of man, yet we are more spiritually malnourished than ever before. We're eating food for sure; it's just not the spiritual food we need to grow up in our salvation as followers of Jesus. We feast on sitcoms, Facebook, Hollywood, romance novels, materialism, pleasure, and a host of other delicacies this world prepares for all who come to the table. The problem is that when we devour these items on the world's menu, we lose our appetite for real nourishment.

It reminds me of the work we do in Guatemala. Did you know that Guatemala has the highest percentage of childhood malnutrition in the Western Hemisphere? It's not that children don't have food. It's simply that they have the wrong kind of food with no or very little nutritional content. Spiritually speaking, it's much like how many believers try to live their Christian lives. Yes, they eat, but what they eat doesn't help them grow up in their salvation.

A malnourished child is a heartbreaking site. I have seen many of them during my trips to Guatemala over the years. A malnourished believer in Jesus is a heartbreaking site as well. I have seen many of them in over thirty years of ministry. As a spiritual parent, I beg you to eat what God has prepared for you so you can grow and experience the salvation Jesus died on a cross to give you. It's so much more than an eternity. There is a transformed life you are missing out on. There is a richness that comes with spiritual maturity you are missing out on. There are purposes and plans He has designed for you to experience. There is an adventure in joining Him to make a difference in this world. All this comes from feeding on His word? Absolutely! Look at what His word will do in you.

Second Timothy 3:16–17 says, "All Scripture is God-breathed and is useful for teaching, rebuking, correcting and training in righteousness, so that the servant of God may be thoroughly equipped for every good work." The food is at your fingertips. Don't you think it's time to develop that craving for the spiritual milk God has given you? Your growth is at stake.

Scripture for the Day:

Psalm 119

Thought for the Day:

As you read Psalm 119, notice all the benefits that come from the word of God. Have you developed the habit of reading the word of God every day? Would you like these benefits to become your reality?

SPIRITUAL MALNUTRITION

We do a lot of work in Guatemala. We work in several schools, one of which we helped to establish. We have our own sponsorship program, in which people can help a child go to school, get an education, learn about Jesus, and get something nutritious to eat. In Guatemala, it's not that they have a food shortage; they have a nutrition problem. Guatemala ranks number one in childhood malnutrition, out of all countries in the Western Hemisphere. We see the results of malnutrition every time we go. We see the physical stunting; we see how a lack of nutrition impacts cognitive development; and we see how it impacts the overall health of a child. Malnutrition is a real and serious problem.

Just as physical malnutrition negatively impacts lives, so does spiritual malnutrition. When people give their lives to Jesus Christ, they are spiritually born. A new spiritual life has begun. This new life must be nurtured and cared for just like a physical life. Unfortunately, so many followers of Jesus are critically malnourished. They lack the necessary nutrition to grow and become strong and capable followers of Jesus.

Second Peter 2:2–3 says, "Like newborn babies, crave pure spiritual milk, so that by it you may grow up in your salvation, now that you have tasted that the Lord is good." What is this spiritual milk the author is referring to? It is the nutritious drink of the word of God. The word of God is spiritual food for the follower of Jesus; it is an absolutely essential nutrient for growth and development. Without the continual consumption of the word of God, the follower of Jesus will be spiritually weak, anemic, and powerless in this fallen world. It is God's word that helps us grow in the salvation we started. It is a spiritual fact that you cannot become all God desires you to be spiritually without His word. The reason so many believers in Jesus simply cannot live out their faith in this dark world is due more to spiritual malnutrition than to a rebellious nature. Most people lack the spiritual stamina this life requires because they have neglected the necessary nutrients to grow strong.

I have talked to so many people over the years who simply don't want to read God's word and struggle to find the motivation to read God's word. They certainly don't "crave" it like a newborn craves milk. They allow these feelings to dictate their spiritual diets. We need to address this issue as we would our physical diets. What do I mean? Every meal I eat isn't a "bell ringer." I absolutely love a good steak or a mouth-watering feast of baby back ribs, but to expect every meal to be like this isn't reality. Sometimes I eat because I need to. Sometimes I eat because my body needs it. Often I'm in a hurry, and I slam down a quick bowl of cereal. Sometimes a quick sandwich or salad will have to do. If I go without a meal, I lose energy and mental focus, which impacts what I want to do.

When it comes to reading God's word and feeding spiritually on its nutrition, we need to have the same mentality. Every spiritual meal isn't going to be a "bell ringer," yet the meal is important. Often we have unrealistic expectations when we read the word of God. We expect it to leap off the page, profoundly impact our emotions, or radically challenge our thinking. Maybe we expect it to always make us feel better. We let our emotions determine the effectiveness of reading the Bible instead of resting on the fact that we need to continually feed on its truth. I don't let my feelings dictate my physical diet. Why do we allow our feelings dictate our spiritual diet?

If you read God's word and don't "feel" anything, it's okay. My bowl of oatmeal this morning didn't give me an emotional rush either. Sometimes mealtime is like that. Sometimes spiritual mealtime is like that as well. But that fact doesn't change the truth that we need to be in God's word daily, feeding our minds, souls, and spirits with its supernatural truth, which has the power to transform us. If you have given up on reading God's word daily, maybe today is the day to begin again. Trust the word of God, not what you feel. God's word is having an impact on your life, whether you can feel it or not. Don't let yourself become spiritually malnourished.

Scripture for the Day:

2 Timothy 3:16–17

Thought for the Day:

Have you allowed what you feel to dictate your spiritual diet? How can you begin to develop the habit of feeding on God's word every day?

THE POWER OF GOD'S WORD

Every once in a while, during winter, we get a powerful windstorm that knocks out power for a few hours to several days. During these times I am reminded of how dependent we are on power. We need power for everything. Without it we have no heat, no lights, no microwave or stove, no running water (we have a well), no TV, and no coffee maker. How I praise God for camping equipment during these times and, of course, my camp coffeepot. You never want to face a power outage without a good pot of coffee. Power is one of those necessities of life.

Power is also a necessity for the follower of Jesus. We need power to live this life. Thankfully, power is promised and provided in the word of God. The Bible is actually a supernaturally empowered book. Yes, there is definitely power in the word of God. Many people simply view it as a collection of writings that show us how to live, but it is so much more than that. There is power in this book. If you desire more power to live this life, then spending time in the Bible is the place to begin. Why do I say this? Just consider the ten following statements about the Bible:

God's word has power because it came from God:
- Second Tim. 3:16 says, "All Scripture is God-breathed."
- Second Peter 1:20–21 says, "Above all, you must understand that no prophecy of Scripture came about by the prophet's own interpretation of things. For prophecy never had its origin in the human will, but prophets, though human, spoke from God as they were carried along by the Holy Spirit."

God's word has power to determine motives:
- Hebrews 4:12 says, "For the word of God is alive and active. Sharper than any double-edged sword, it penetrates even to dividing soul and spirit, joints and marrow; it judges the thoughts and attitudes of the heart."

God's word has power to overcome temptation:

- Matthew 4:3–4 says, "The tempter came to him and said, 'If you are the Son of God, tell these stones to become bread.' Jesus answered, 'It is written: "Man shall not live on bread alone, but on every word that comes from the mouth of God."'"

God's word has power to defeat Satan:

- Ephesians 6:17 says, "Take the helmet of salvation and the sword of the Spirit, which is the word of God."

God's word has power to provide success:

- Joshua 1:8 says, "Keep this Book of the Law always on your lips; meditate on it day and night, so that you may be careful to do everything written in it. Then you will be prosperous and successful."

God's word has power to equip us for service:

- Second Timothy 3:16–17 says. "All Scripture is God-breathed and is useful for teaching, rebuking, correcting and training in righteousness, so that the servant of God may be thoroughly equipped for every good work."

God's word has power to set us free from sin:

- John 17:17 says, "Sanctify them by the truth; your word is truth."

God's word has power to give us direction in life:

- Psalm 119:105 says, "Your word is a lamp for my feet, a light on my path."

God's word has power to revive our emotions:

- Psalm 119:92 says, "If your law had not been my delight, I would have perished in my affliction."

God's word has power to save:

- Romans 1:16 says, "For I am not ashamed of the gospel, because it is the power of God that brings salvation to everyone who believes: first to the Jew, then to the Gentile."

Who doesn't need more power to live this life? At your fingertips is a book filled with power. Its power has changed the course of human history, and it is still transforming lives today. What about you? Have you allowed the word of God to become powerful in your life? Have you tasted this power that is available to you? It's time to explore the mysteries of a book that has been at your fingertips all this time.

Scripture for the Day:

Reflect on each of the above verses.

Thought for the Day:

Have you ever looked at the Bible as a book of power? What is your perspective of the Bible? How does this belief impact your relationship with this amazing book?

STOLEN IDENTITY

Have you ever had someone steal your identity? Oh my, what a pain! A few years ago, we had someone steal our credit card number three times. Identity theft is big business these days. Over twelve million people every year have their identities stolen. If you've been a victim to this crime, I feel your pain.

Identity theft, however, is nothing new. Identity theft has been going on since the beginning of creation. In fact, we gave up our true identity in the garden of Eden. Satan deceived us into giving up our real identities, and we traded the ones God created us with for a fallen version. Our identities have been stolen, and it is time to get them back. We have allowed the world to define who we are, we've allowed our failures to define who we are, we've allowed others to tell us who we are, and we've allowed Satan to lie to us about who we really are. When we believe comments about ourselves that aren't true, our identities are being stolen.

Why is this so important? Because you live what you believe. If your identity is founded in your performance, job, money, success, looks, possessions, popularity, or failures, you will always struggle with your self-worth. Why? Because you can never be good enough, rich enough, successful enough, beautiful enough, or popular enough in this life to satisfy your longing for worth. And if what I am is never enough, I will always struggle with my self-worth. If this is how you feel today, then your identity has been stolen. It is time for you to believe that you are who God says you are and get your identity back. But how? By believing who God says you are.

God Says I Am Made in His Image:
- Genesis 1:27 says, "So God created mankind in his own image, in the image of God he created them; male and female he created them."

God Says I Am His Marvelous Workmanship:

- Psalm 139:13–14 says, "For you created my inmost being; you knit me together in my mother's womb. I praise you because I am fearfully and wonderfully made; your works are wonderful; I know that full well."

God Says I Am His Dearly Loved Child:

- Romans 8:38–39 says, "For I am convinced that neither death nor life, neither angels nor demons, neither the present nor the future, nor any powers, neither height nor depth, nor anything else in all creation, will be able to separate us from the love of God that is in Christ Jesus our Lord."

God Says I Am Worth Dying For:

- John 3:16 says, "For God so loved the world that he gave his one and only Son, that whoever believes in him shall not perish but have eternal life."
- Romans 5:8 says, "But God demonstrates his own love for us in this: While we were still sinners, Christ died for us."

God Says I Am Created for Victory:

- Romans 8:37 says, "No, in all these things we are more than conquerors through him who loved us."
- First Corinthians 15:57 says, "But thanks be to God! He gives us the victory through our Lord Jesus Christ."

God Says I Am Created for Purpose

- Ephesians 2:10 says, "For we are God's handiwork, created in Christ Jesus to do good works, which God prepared in advance for us to do."

It's easy to allow our identities to be stolen. We are prone to become blinded to who we really are. Life gets hard. We are overcome by our failures and brokenness. Our lives sometimes just don't measure up to our expectations. We experience pain and crisis. Pretty soon all these circumstances begin to define who we are. We start believing the lies that we will never measure up. We see ourselves through the lens of disappointment and unrealized expectations. All we see are broken relationships, shattered dreams, and an unsure future. We hear the voice of the enemy telling us it's hopeless.

You have a choice. You can listen to what your enemy says about you or choose to listen to the voice of the God who made you. You can allow your identity to be founded in some disappointing circumstance or unmet expectation of this life, or you can choose to let it be founded in who God says you are. Yes, you can get your identity back. You do have a choice. Your true identity is your right and privilege of being a child of the living God. In Jesus' name, go take it back. God Himself gave it to you. The enemy has no power to keep it if you choose to claim it. Now go claim what is rightfully yours!

Scripture for the Day:

Reflect on the above scriptures and notice which ones impact you the most.

Thought for the Day:

Go stand in front of a mirror and read each statement aloud with the scripture that goes with it. Do you struggle doing this? Why? Is it difficult accepting these six truths about yourself? Say these statements daily until they become normal, everyday beliefs.

GOD'S WILL FOR YOUR LIFE: THANKFULNESS

First Thessalonians 5:18 says, "Give thanks in all circumstances; for this is God's will for you in Christ Jesus."

Let's be honest. Thankfulness is easier said than done. It's hard to be thankful all the time. I realize that being thankful is one of the marks of a follower of Jesus, but this life is so broken and dark that being thankful can be a challenge. I also realize that being thankful is God's will for me, but I still find myself struggling to give thanks when the circumstances are painful and my heart is broken and disappointed. Maybe this is where you find yourself today. The relentless waves of painful circumstances have taken their toll on your heart, and being thankful just seems completely out of your reach. You may be thinking, *How can I possibly be thankful?*

Learning to be thankful is realizing that thankfulness isn't tied to circumstances but to the character of God. Psalm 106:1 says, "Praise the Lord. Give thanks to the Lord, for he is good; His love endures forever." Notice that the reason for praise and thanks is in who God is.

Our barrier with being thankful often lies in our thinking. We mentally and emotionally connect being thankful only with favorable circumstances. Now, there is nothing wrong with thanking God for things that work out well. I have had some amazing days of sturgeon and salmon fishing on the Willamette River. The weather was great, the fishing was successful, and the company was encouraging. It's easy to thank God when everything goes according to our expectations. But this is real life, and not everything always goes well. In fact, many times the circumstances are downright discouraging. Yet God still wants us to learn how to be thankful in all circumstances. I might not always be thankful for all circumstances, but I can choose to be thankful in the midst of them. How? When I remember that the foundation of my thankful heart is grounded in who God is, not in my circumstances. My circumstances always change. God never changes. My circumstances aren't always good, but God is always good.

Becoming a thankful person in all circumstances is a relational thing. It depends on our understanding of who God is. The more you understand who God is, the more you can be thankful. The less you understand God, the more your heart will be simply tied to favorable circumstances. Because I believe God is always good, unconditionally loves me, is forever faithful, has my best interest in mind, will graciously provide for my needs, can use every event for His good purposes, and promises to reward obedience, I can be thankful in Him no matter what.

I don't believe circumstance is the driving force of my life. I believe God is. Therefore, even in circumstances I don't like and maybe even hate, I can be thankful that God is bigger than that circumstance. Do you see why being thankful is a relational process and not merely about circumstances?

If you are in the midst of circumstances that are hard, painful, and overwhelming, what do you believe about God? This is why being thankful is so important. The pain of this life can cause us to question the very character of God. If His character is eroded in our minds, then so will be the relationship. There have been times in the darkest, most painful moments of my life when I chose to praise God for His goodness, even though nothing in my life was good at the time. With tears streaming down my face, I have cried, "God, I still believe You are good. I still choose to thank You despite the darkness in my life." You may be thinking, *What good did that do? How did that change anything?* It didn't change one thing about my circumstances, but it changed me profoundly. Maybe it's time to look at that painful circumstance that is in your path, blocking your view of God, and declare God's faithfulness to its face. Will it change the circumstance? Probably not. Will it change you? Why don't you follow Jesus and find out?

Scripture for the Day:

Psalm 50:23; 107:22; Philippians 2:14–15

Thought for the Day:

Does a thankful heart define your life? Do you spend more time thinking about and expressing your thankfulness or more time and mental energy complaining and wishing that things were different? Which do you think Jesus would have you do? How will you choose to be thankful today?

CHAPTER 6

MOVING AHEAD
FOLLOWING JESUS

PARADOX OF THE SURRENDERED LIFE

When I was little boy, our family lived on a farm. The farm had crops, cattle, chickens, and a host of other things little boys love. Some things in particular we had an abundance of were barn cats. There was this one huge tomcat that was the most affectionate thing you ever did see. He'd come around the house, and my older brother loved to pick him up and pack him around. The only dilemma to this match made in heaven was that my brother was too little, and the cat was too big for him to carry him properly. He'd put that cat in a loving headlock, and away they'd go. My parents would catch them together like that time and time again, and would worry about the cat's safety. That cat never seemed to struggle, though. One fateful day when my brother walked around the side of the house, holding the cat, it seemed a bit lifeless. Sure enough, he had loved this poor cat to death. He had held the poor cat so tight that it was now in "kitty heaven."

Now, I know many of you are horrified by this story. Let me just say that no cats have been harmed since. But this does illustrate a very important spiritual principle. You're thinking, *What could this possibly represent?* If we hold on to our lives too tightly, we will destroy them as well. There is a very important paradox Jesus talked about that we must come to understand if we are serious about following Him. Luke 9:23–24 says, "Then he said to them all: 'Whoever wants to be my disciple must deny themselves and take up their cross daily and follow me. For whoever wants to save their life will lose it, but whoever loses their life for me will save it.'"

Did you catch this? If we try to hang on to our lives, we will lose them. If we give up our lives, we will save them. Do you see the paradox? Jesus came to give us life to the fullest (John 10:10), but so often His followers never realized this life. Why? Often the answer lies in our unwillingness to give up our lives. In following Jesus there is an exchange that takes place. If we give up our lives, Jesus will in turn give us a new life in its place. He pours His life into us. The reason we don't experience this new life is that our lives haven't been surrendered first. Our lives are still so full of "us" that we cannot be filled with Jesus. How can Jesus fill something that is already full? How can Jesus bring a resurrected new life to someone who has yet to die?

I realize it feels very unnatural to give up your life. But this is what Jesus calls His followers to do. The more we try to "save" our own lives, the more our lives keep slipping away. Maybe it's time to embrace the paradox of the surrendered life. Why not sacrifice the life you can't save anyway for the one Jesus gives you, the one that can never be lost?

Scripture for the Day:

Romans12:1–2; 1 Corinthians 6:19–20

Thought for the Day:

What is keeping you from truly surrendering your life to Jesus? Imagine what your life would be like if you embraced this paradox.

CHARACTER OR COMFORT?

We have become a society addicted to our personal comfort. We want more comfort in our homes, in our vehicles, at our jobs, in our shopping, and with our electronics. There's an app for that, right? There's nothing wrong with comfort in and of itself. The problem comes when we trade character for comfort. The issue comes when we value and pursue comfort over and above character; then we begin to travel down a slippery slope. When our personal comfort becomes our highest ethic, we're in trouble.

Proverbs is a book filled with short, pithy statements of truth. Many of these statements are contrasting character versus comfort. Many try to illustrate the end result of each pursuit. Consider the following verses from Proverbs 28. "When a country is rebellious, it has many rulers, but a ruler with discernment and knowledge maintains order" (v. 2).

Moral rot is the result of pursuing comfort. Wisdom and knowledge are the results of pursuing character. "Better the poor whose walk is blameless than the rich whose ways are perverse" (v. 6).

Dishonesty to acquire riches is an issue of pursuing comfort. Being willing to have less and be honest is the result of character. How many of you would rather be poor and honest? "A faithful person will be richly blessed, but one eager to get rich will not go unpunished" (v. 20).

People who want to get rich quickly are pursuers of comfort. A person known for being trustworthy is a person of character.

As followers of Jesus, we should be known as people of character. We may enjoy many of the comforts of our culture and the blessings from all our technology, but pursuers of comfort we are not. We would rather be known for our character in a dark, broken world than any material comfort we have attained. To sacrifice our character on the altar of comfort and convenience is to deny the Savior we claim to follow. If we desire God's blessing, then we must be people who value character over comfort.

Proverbs 2:7–8 says, "He holds success in store for the upright, he is a shield to those whose walk is blameless, for He guards the course of the just and protects the way of his faithful ones."

Did you notice all the benefits and blessings from those who embrace character? Don't believe the lies that come from the messengers of comfort. The real blessings in this life don't come from trying to figure out how to make our lives more comfortable and experience a life of ease. The real blessings will always come from a life of godly character by following Jesus.

Scripture for the Day:

What day of the month is it? Read that chapter number in the book of Proverbs.

Thought for the Day:

Let's be brutally honest. If you had a choice to compromise your character, knowing it would benefit you in some way, such as finances, job promotion, or house application, what would you do? What if being honest actually harmed you in some way? Character or comfort?

ETERNAL HOPE

It's so easy to try to create heaven on earth. Why do I say this? Because we are a culture obsessed with comfort and convenience. We have an obsession with working ourselves to death by trying to make our lives more comfortable. (Do you see the irony of this?) We want more comfort in our homes. We want more comfort at our employment. We want more comfort in our retirement. We want the latest piece of technology so we can experience how it makes our lives more convenient. We want comfort and convenience in relationships. Why do I say this? Because of how quickly we dispose of them when they get difficult. When things aren't comfortable and convenient, we actually feel like something is wrong in this life.

As followers of Jesus in this broken world, it is imperative that we have our hope fixed on eternity. This world is never going to be comfortable or convenient in the way our hearts truly long for. This world is broken. This world is under the control of the evil one. This world is dark. We are commanded not to love this world or the things it offers us. Often the reason we struggle so much with hope in this world is that we expect benefits from this life that only eternity will bring. We try to create heaven on earth. This is a fruitless and exasperating exercise. The followers of Jesus have their hope fixed somewhere else. We know this world isn't our true home. We are citizens of an eternal kingdom, and we know that true comfort and convenience are coming later in eternity, not in this life.

> But our citizenship is in heaven. And we eagerly await a Savior from there, the Lord Jesus Christ. (Phil. 3:20)

> For we know that if the earthly tent we live in is destroyed, we have a building from God, an eternal house in heaven, not built by human hands. Meanwhile

> we groan, longing to be clothed instead with our
> heavenly dwelling. (2 Cor. 5:1–2)

> When the perishable has been clothed with the
> imperishable, and the mortal with immortality, then the
> saying that is written will come true: "Death has been
> swallowed up in victory. Where, O death, is your victory?
> Where, O death, is your sting?" (1 Cor. 15:54–55)

We grow weary in our present bodies. The older we get, the more we realize that the comfort and convenience we longed for in this life are a myth. This life is hard. It is often a struggle fraught with discouraging circumstances and the slow deterioration of our own physical bodies. This is why we have an eternal hope. There is something amazing waiting for us. This life doesn't define us, but rather eternity does. If all our hope is anchored merely in this life, we are setting ourselves up for profound disappointment. We can't create heaven on earth. We were never designed to find our hope here. The more you love this world, the less hope you will experience in anticipating eternity. The more you find your hope in anticipating eternity, the less you will love this world.

Where is your hope anchored today? Are you working yourself to death trying to create a fictitious "heaven" here on earth so you can be very comfortable and experience all the conveniences this world has to offer? Is your hope in the American dream or in your true citizenship of an eternal kingdom? In this kingdom, death has no sting, and sin has no power. Our bodies have been transformed from weakness to eternal strength. Relationships are perfect and eternal. All the longings of your heart, which have gone unsatisfied in this life, are now fulfilled and overflowing. The best part is that we get to see Jesus face-to-face. No more taking things by faith anymore. Now our eyes will finally see the One where our faith has been anchored in all these years. Now that's hope.

Scripture for the Day:

Revelation 21:1–7

Thought for the Day:

How much hope do you experience by thinking about what awaits you in eternity? Instead of placing all your hope in this temporary life, why not reflect on what scripture promises will be awaiting you when this life is done?

SOURCE OF COURAGE

When I was in grade school, some of my teachers allowed me to do errands for them. I could get out of class to make copies, go to the library for them, deliver a message to the office, or go get some art supplies. They would give me the all-important hall pass. The hall pass let every other adult know I was representing my teacher; I was on an assignment for her. This was very important, because the principal and I struggled a bit in our relationship—if you know what I mean. Once I had the hall pass, I was filled with courage, even in the face of the principal. In fact, once while I was walking through the hallways, the principal and I met. He quickly and firmly asked me what I was doing out of class. I didn't say a word (which was very unusual for me) and flashed the hall pass. He shook his head in disgust and kept walking. I was brimming with confidence. A twelve-year-old just had shut the principal down.

What's my point? Our courage to live in this world and follow Jesus comes from knowing whom we represent and in whose authority we walk. We represent Jesus in this life. We are His representatives to a dark, dying world. We walk in His authority. He has given us His hall pass for this life so we can live with courage. Our courage doesn't come from within ourselves; it emerges from knowing whom we represent. Second Corinthians 5:20 says, "We are therefore Christ's ambassadors, as though God were making his appeal through us. We implore you on Christ's behalf: Be reconciled to God."

This is why there was a teenage shepherd boy in the Old Testament who could courageously stand before a giant, who was almost ten feet tall, and confidently say,

> You come against me with sword and spear and javelin, but I come against you in the name of the Lord Almighty, the God of the armies of Israel, whom you

have defied. This day the Lord will deliver you into my hands, and I'll strike you down and cut off your head. This very day I will give the carcasses of the Philistine army to the birds and the wild animals, and the whole world will know that there is a God in Israel. All those gathered here will know that it is not by sword or spear that the Lord saves; for the battle is the Lord's, and he will give all of you into our hands. (1 Sam. 17:45–47)

David knew whom he represented, and that conviction gave him courage to face the giant, Goliath.

Are you living life by not realizing whom you represent? You are an ambassador for Christ in this life. You are authorized and empowered to live out Jesus' will here on earth. You carry with you His authority, name, will, interests, presence, and power. Knowing whom you represent is everything. The enemy wants you to live in fear, sneaking through the hallways of life as if you don't belong. It's time for you to show the hall pass Jesus gave you. You are His ambassador. It is time to find courage in your marriage, in your parenting, at your job, in your neighborhood, and even in the face of whatever crisis you may be experiencing. Remind yourself and the enemy of whom you represent. Jesus has given you authority to live in this world. Now choose to live courageously today as one Jesus Himself has authorized.

Scripture for the Day:

Joshua 1:6–9

Thought for the Day:

How much does fear influence your life? Are you trying to find courage within yourself or in knowing whom you represent?

WHO'S YOUR BOSS?

One of the places my wife and I love to snorkel is in the Riviera Maya. This is the stretch of shoreline south of Cancun, Mexico. One such place is the tiny town of Akumal. Here you can snorkel with turtles, stingrays, barracudas, squid, and an assortment of other tropical fish up close. A few years ago, as we were walking down to the beach next to the snorkel equipment rental station, the workers began to yell at us. I ignored them. It's Mexico after all. Finally, they tried English, and I began to pay a bit more attention. They told us we had to get our equipment from them to snorkel on the beach. We graciously held up our own gear as we walked. Then they barked that we had to rent life jackets from them to snorkel at the beach. We graciously kept walking, found a nice palm tree to camp under, put on our snorkel gear, and said hi to the turtles. Why did we ignore them? They were lying. They had no authority and were giving out misleading information simply to take advantage of people. They weren't the bosses of the beach.

As we follow Jesus on this faith journey, we are going to hear many competing voices besides our Shepherd's. We are going to hear the voice of this world, our fallen humanity, and the devil. All are trying to boss us around, tell us where to go, and try to limit our freedom we have in Christ. Often they want us to pay for things Christ has freely given to us. It's imperative for us to realize who we are, who we follow, and what authority we have as followers of Jesus.

> For sin shall no longer be your master, because you are not under the law, but under grace. (Rom. 6:14)

> What, then, shall we say in response to these things? If God is for us, who can be against us? (Rom. 8:31)

> See to it that no one takes you captive through hollow and deceptive philosophy, which depends on human tradition and the elemental spiritual forces of this world rather than on Christ. (Col. 2:8)

> Since you died with Christ to the elemental spiritual forces of this world, why, as though you still belonged to the world, do you submit to its rules? (Col. 2:20)

Let's be clear: sin and our fallen humanity are no longer our masters. Satan lost all authority at the cross. The world with all its influence isn't our home or our love. God is for us, not against us. Nothing can separate us from the love of Christ. Jesus is our boss, and no one else is. Therefore, ignore these other voices you hear trying to create fear, misdirection, and confusion. Keep walking and tune your eyes and ears to Jesus. These other voices will yell, scream, demand obedience, and try to intimidate you into compliance. Ignore them. Walk forward in the freedom, authority, and love of Jesus. The only power and authority these other voices have are what you give them. Jesus set you free from their tyranny. It's your choice whether you live in it.

Scripture for the Day:

Colossians 2:13–15

Thought for the Day:

How have you been allowing sin, rather than Jesus, to be your boss? How have you been allowing the world to be your boss? How are you allowing Satan to boss you around? How can you ignore these voices and listen only to Jesus?

FOLLOWING JESUS IS MESSY

My granddaughter is just learning to walk. She crawls over to the couch or a chair, grabs hold of whatever she can, and then confidently stands to her feet in triumph with a big smile. All is well while she hangs on to something. As soon as she lets go and tries to move those little legs and feet forward, down she goes. Most of the time this process is entertaining and uneventful. But there are those times when on her descent she hits her head or takes a face-plant on the floor. There are crying, tears, embracing, and the ever-encouraging words from Mom, Dad, and Grandpa and Grandma to try again. The amazing thing to watch is that she never gets discouraged, no matter how often she falls. It's as if she knows those legs are supposed to do more than this, and she'll keep trying until she's got it. Falling is simply part of learning to walk.

I don't know why we lose this perspective as we get older. Who does anything perfect the first time? Falling is part of learning to walk. Why do we think following Jesus is any different? Why do we think we should have this walking-with-Jesus thing down pat as soon as we give our lives to Him? Does anything in life work this way? Nothing I've discovered does. Yet often the church community expects people to be "cleaned up" more than they really are. They expect people to fail less than they really do. So many followers of Jesus are weighed down with guilt because they can't walk successfully, following Jesus. The truth of the matter is that following Jesus is messy. Why? Learning to follow Jesus involves failure.

Please understand that I'm not trying to make excuses for sinful behavior. I'm simply trying to describe a reality I have seen for years. Growth takes time, and growth is messy. Even though we have the desire to walk forward, many times we still take a face-plant. We stood up with confidence, only to find ourselves sprawled out on the ground once again. Haven't you ever felt like this? Even the apostle Paul described this dilemma.

> I do not understand what I do. For what I want to do I do not do, but what I hate I do. (Rom. 7:15)

> For I have the desire to do what is good, but I cannot carry it out. (Rom. 7:18)

For those of you who are discouraged because you feel that you're never going to get this spiritual walking figured out, take heart. Falling is part of the process. Jesus has taken care of the falling part. He died on a cross for your sin. He paid the price for your falling. Falling doesn't surprise Him. Falling doesn't make Him avoid you. Falling doesn't cause Him to abandon you. He has more than enough grace, mercy, and patience for the time it takes for you to learn how to walk in step with Him.

I know some people reading this are so discouraged that they want to quit. Maybe you have quit. Maybe you've listened to the judgmental voices of the stone throwers who are ready to condemn with rocks in their hands. Please don't allow these voices to determine your future relationship with Jesus. There's another voice calling to you. Do you hear it? It's Jesus. He's saying, "That's okay. I still love you. I died for that failure." "Now get back up and hold My hand this time." "Let Me help you learn to walk." "Let Me show you how to depend on Me." "When you fall again—and you will—the quicker you take My hand again, the quicker you and I walk again." "I love you more than your failures." "Please don't quit."

To truly learn to follow Jesus can be a messy process lined with failures, but the effort is worth it. To learn how to spiritually walk, run, and even sprint with Jesus in this life is worth it all. Are you ready? It's time to try again.

Scripture for the Day:

Philippians. 3:12–14

Thought for the Day:

Don't allow your past failures to define your future progress. Are you focused on the past, or are you pressing forward to what Jesus has in store for you?

GUARD YOUR HEART

In our western, rational way of looking at life, we sometimes neglect our hearts. What do I mean? We like to deal with life in a cognitive way. We reason, we process mentally, we create a linear way of accomplishing things, and we value ourselves as rational people. As important as our thinking process is, though, our hearts drive our lives. Our hearts actually have more influence than our thoughts do. Now, before you all disagree with me, listen to the word of God.

Proverbs 4:23 says, "Above all else, guard your heart, for everything you do flows from it."

Of course our thinking has tremendous influence on our lives. Even our ongoing transformation in Jesus is connected to allowing God to transform the way we think (Rom. 12:2). But our hearts are the motivation. Our hearts are the power. From our hearts come the passion, the fire, and the determination for life. Our hearts are the engine for life while our minds are the rudder. What our hearts burn for will determine, more than our thoughts, the course of our lives. Sometimes our hearts can get so passionate about something that our minds can no longer steer or control direction. It's like driving your car too fast, and you can't make the corner. You simply have too much speed. Our hearts can be like this.

Why do I say this? Haven't we all mentally known we should do something, but then we don't do it? *Why wasn't my thinking enough to dictate the course?* Maybe you started doing the right thing but couldn't maintain it. Why? Thinking alone doesn't determine the course of your life. Your heart does! If your heart isn't engaged and committed to whatever your mind has agreed on, the heart will eventually win every time. If you're highly disciplined, you may be able to make yourself do things your heart doesn't want to do for some time, but eventually your heart will win. Why do people have affairs when they know such behavior is wrong? Why do people gossip when they know doing so wounds others? Why do young people marry someone they obviously shouldn't? This is a matter of the heart, not the mind.

There seems to be so much attention today in Christian circles about guarding our minds—and rightfully so. But I don't hear too much about guarding our hearts. I think this is because guarding one's heart is a much more subjective topic. Guarding your mind is more objective. I can talk about media, porn, romance novels, movies, what we read, the music we listen to, and the importance of reading our Bibles. But matters of the heart are messier. Our hearts are part of our personalities, our identities, our uniqueness, and what makes us tick. My heart may be drawn to things your heart is not. I may have to guard my heart from things that aren't an issue for you. It's just not a simple matter.

So how do we guard our hearts? Let me give you some simple considerations. Pay attention to what you're drawn to. Be aware of what lights up passion in you. Take notice of what things create your inner motivation. Those are heart issues. Now compare them to God's word. *Are these issues I need to avoid? Why would I avoid them if they create motivation in me?* They might be creating motivation for something God tells us to stay away from. Increased exposure to things that light your heart up in the wrong direction will only connect your heart more to the wrong thing. This works in the negative and the positive way. Increased exposure to the right things that light up your heart increases passion for godly actions. Going to Guatemala year after year, serving needy people, only increases my passion to make a difference in their lives. My heart connects more deeply with increased exposure.

Increased exposure to pursuing the things of this world will cause our hearts to be attached to it. In essence, we will begin loving these worldly things. When we increase our worldly exposure and diminish our relational exposure with God, our hearts naturally follow. We can mentally tell ourselves all day long that these things are wrong, but now that our hearts are connected, love trumps the mind every time, even if it's love for the wrong thing.

These are issues we need to be aware of and guard ourselves against. Are you guarding your heart? First John 2:15 says, "Do not love the world or anything in the world. If anyone loves the world, love for the Father is not in them."

I've heard people say, "How could they do that when they know it's wrong?" It's easy; it's a heart issue. Be careful not to be too judgmental of others. The reality is, we all struggle with the same issue of allowing our hearts to be drawn to the wrong things. We all need to heed this exhortation: "Above all else, guard your heart, for everything you do flows from it." (Prov. 4:23). What course has your heart set you on?

Scripture for the Day:

Mark 7:17–23

Thought for the Day:

Are there things you have allowed your heart to become attached to that may draw you away from Jesus? How do you need to guard your heart?

LIVE YOUR SEASON

Some of the things I love about living in the Pacific Northwest are the distinct seasons we get to enjoy. Some places don't share this seasonal characteristic. If you live somewhere a bit more tropical, this simply isn't your reality. Yet for those of us who live a bit farther north of the equator, knowing what season you're in makes all the difference in the world. Why? Our behavior follows the specific seasons. Where I live, you don't plant your garden in January. You don't typically go camping in March unless your desire is for rain to drown you. Fall is for hunting. Spring is for fishing. Summer tends to be the time for vacations. Our seasons influence our behavior and choices.

Not only do we have seasons in nature, but we also have seasons in life. As I look back on my life, I see very distinct seasons. There was that season of being newly married, which was filled with discovery and freedom with just the two of us. There was that season of having kids. Oh my, did that change the climate! The seasons certainly changed. There was the season when our kids were in school. That was a long season for sure, with many microclimates along the way, as they transitioned from elementary school through high school. There was that young adult season as they were going to school, living at home, and figuring out life as adults. There was the season when they got married, and Lisa and I found ourselves as "empty nesters." Now we are in one of the greatest seasons of all, the season of being grandparents. Yes, it is *that* awesome! With each season come very specific behaviors and choices.

Ecclesiastes 3:1 says, "There is a time for everything, and a season for every activity under the heavens." The word of God agrees that life is filled with seasons. It is therefore imperative for us to understand what season we're in and then adjust our lives to be successful in that particular one. Why? Because failure to live in your season is to forfeit that season forever. You and I can never get it back. Once a season is past, it is gone. Unlike the four seasons of the Pacific Northwest, which repeat every year, our lives are filled with many seasons that don't repeat year after year. Therefore, clarity in your season is critical.

Not only is clarity essential, but acceptance is too. Do you accept the season you're in? I may not particularly like January in Oregon, but I accept the fact that it's winter. Constantly wishing it was July will only make me miserable in January. I see many people living this way. They constantly complain about the season they're in and therefore make themselves miserable in that season. Let's face it: some seasons are simply harder than others. You might be in a hard season right now. Continually wishing you didn't have to experience this season will only make it worse. Instead, look at the season and understand what it requires from you. Accept this responsibility and choose to live in that season.

There were times when Lisa and I were in very hard financial seasons. This situation required us to tell ourselves no often and learn to be content with the little we had. There were seasons when both of our girls were little and in diapers, and both needed constant attention from their mom and dad. That season was hard and required us to make specific choices to live the season well. We had seasons when our kids were in sports, and there were plenty of hours logged on soccer fields and basketball courts. With each new season came changes, transitions, and specific choices to live in the season we found ourselves in.

I know you are in a specific season right now. It may be a pleasant one or a difficult one. The pleasant ones are easy to live in. It's the seasons of struggle and hardship that are tough. If the latter is you, can I encourage you to embrace the season you're in? Yes, it is hard, but in this season God is still with you. He is teaching you lessons you will need for upcoming seasons. There are relational dynamics in this season you can never replay. There is refining in this season that will produce a greater appreciation for future seasons.

Finally, sometimes winter can seem to last forever. The dark days often feel endless here in the Northwest, but eventually winter gives way to spring. Warmth and life return, and the seasons begin to change. The season you're in won't last forever either. This is a season; it isn't your life. Your life won't be defined by your current climate. Trust me, it will change. The best thing you can do is live in the season you're in, asking God to give you the grace for however long the season lasts. Even in winter there is still beauty to be found in the harshness of the climate. May God allow you to see the beauty in the season you're in and the strength to live in it.

Scripture for the Day:

Ecclesiastes 3:1–8

Thought for the Day:

Describe the season you're in. What is the best way to live in it? How much time do you spend wishing you were in a different season? Are you allowing this desire to steal your joy?

THE CHURCH ISN'T SUPPOSED TO BE SAFE

Now, before you react to the title, hear me out. Of course, the church is supposed to be a loving, accepting, forgiving, and caring place for individuals. But the church doesn't exist for this. The point of the church isn't to simply create an amazing environment. It is to accomplish a mission while maintaining this environment: the church providing relational safety to people—absolutely; the church providing safety in general—absolutely not! Why do I say this? Jesus never intended for the church to promote a lifestyle of safety. In fact, following Jesus with all your heart, along with a group of others doing the same thing, can be the most dangerous thing you can do.

Several years ago Lisa and I had the privilege of going to Pearl Harbor and touring the battleship *Missouri*. We loved this experience. It was fascinating hearing the history and being able to walk through this impressive World War II battleship. One of the things I noticed was that it wasn't designed for comfort. It was designed for battle. It was created in such a way that it was very difficult to sink. It could withstand multiple hits and remain not only afloat but also still in the battle, dealing out punishment. Everything about this battleship screams "mission." It wasn't designed to be a museum. It was designed to be in the most dangerous places on earth and come out on top when all the smoke cleared. To this day it still has the dents in its massive hull from a kamikaze Zero trying to sink it. This ship wasn't designed for safety. It was designed for combat.

The imagery of the church is much like a battleship. What we've done to the modern-day church has made it more like a cruise ship. Cruise ships are all about comfort, safety and the denial of reality. Yes, I've been on a cruise ship as well. A little denial of reality is good for everyone now and then. But the church is designed to live in the reality of this fallen world, engaging the enemy and accomplishing the mission of sharing the gospel with fallen men and women. This mission is certainly not safe. Jesus calls us to follow Him, and the places where He goes aren't always the safest. Jesus promised hardship, rejection, persecution, and resistance. A promise of safety isn't part of the deal. Following Him wherever He leads us is. Look at the following passages.

> If the world hates you, keep in mind that it hated me first. If you belonged to the world, it would love you as its own. As it is, you do not belong to the world, but I have chosen you out of the world. That is why the world hates you. (John 15:18–19)

> I have told you these things, so that in me you may have peace. In this world you will have trouble. But take heart! I have overcome the world. (John 16:33)

> Then Jesus came to them and said, "All authority in heaven and on earth has been given to me. Therefore go and make disciples of all nations, baptizing them in the name of the Father and of the Son and of the Holy Spirit, and teaching them to obey everything I have commanded you. And surely I am with you always, to the very end of the age." (Matt. 28:18–20)

Following Jesus should be the greatest adventure this life has to offer. It's not your career or your dream vacation but the life of risk and embracing the unknown with Jesus leading the way. Most believers are simply bored out of their minds when it comes to church. Why? Because they are looking for a cruise ship experience. Instead of being challenged by the expansion of the mission, they are obsessed with expanding their comfort. The only program God has for changing this world is the church. He has no other plan. There is no plan B. There is no other agenda but you and me following Jesus in the context of His church.

Now, what about you? Are you looking for your church to provide you with safety? Or are you willing to follow Jesus on an adventure? There is brokenness all around you. There are hurting people everywhere you look. There are people trapped in bondage and despair. The mission screams for participants who are sitting around, waiting for their glasses to be filled, instead of running to the battlefront, following their Captain and Chief. The church isn't supposed to be safe. The church is supposed to be on a mission. Are you?

Scripture for the Day:

2 Corinthians 5:18–20

Thought for the Day:

What are you really looking for in a church? Are you looking for more than relational safety? Are you willing to leave the land of predictability and safety, and embrace the adventure you were destined for?

WHO DEFINES YOU?

I don't know about you, but I can be pretty hard on myself. I have a tendency to feel good about myself when I do what I perceive to be right, good, or maybe even exceptional. If my performance is good, I tend to feel good about myself. On the other hand, there are times when I don't do what is good or right, and I fall far short of exceptional; the resulting feelings are less than complimentary. It doesn't take much for me to begin beating myself up over even minor things. I miss the exit on the freeway; I lose my patience working on my truck; I say an unkind word or use a harsh tone when talking to my wife. I find that I struggle with the reality of being so imperfect. But this is the true condition of our humanity. If we use performance as defining ourselves, we're going to struggle for the rest of our lives. If I use myself as the standard for defining who I am, that becomes a very discouraging prospect.

The good news for those who are followers of Jesus is that we aren't the standard, but Jesus is. The reality is that no matter how good our performance may be at any given time, it will never be enough. Isaiah 64:6 says, "All of us have become like one who is unclean, and all our righteous acts are like filthy rags." You see, it doesn't matter how good you think your performance is or has been; it doesn't matter before God. Everything we can do, no matter how good it is, still looks like filthy rags before God. Some of us performance-oriented people may not like this description, but this is how God sees us. Consider this: Romans 3:10 says, "There is no one righteous, not even one." Even on our best day, we still fall far short of God's expectations. But there is hope.

Ephesians 2:8–10 says, "For it is by grace you have been saved, through faith—and this is not from yourselves, it is the gift of God—not by works, so that no one can boast. For we are God's handiwork, created in Christ Jesus to do good works, which God prepared in advance for us to do." Since God knew our performance could never be good enough, He sent His Son, Jesus, to pay the penalty for our imperfections through His death on the cross. Now, when we accept Jesus and His unconditional forgiveness, our behavior no longer defines who we are, but Jesus does. We are now saved by God's grace poured out on our lives. Our lives are no longer "by works." There is no credit we can take for any of this. Jesus defines our lives on our good days and our bad ones. Our performance is taken out of the equation entirely.

If you are a performance person, you may not like this. Why? Because you feel pretty good about yourself on your good days. You are self-reliant, successful, and goal oriented; and you believe you follow Jesus pretty well. Here's the problem with this. Even on your best day, your performance before God is no better than a filthy rag. That's right. God is not, nor has He ever been, impressed with your performance. The only one who has been impressed by it has been you and a few others. This may sting a little, but it's a pure and simple truth. This perspective allows you to walk in humility before God and others. Without it, you will think more highly of yourself than you should.

Maybe you're the person who is very hard on yourself. You are more than aware of your imperfections, flaws, inconsistencies, and brokenness. You beat yourself up all the time. Your dilemma is that you define yourself by performance as well. The good news for you is this: Jesus defines you on your worst day. The grace that saved you defines you as well. Your performance is taken out of the equation. For you, this gives you hope. You can stop beating yourself up. You can stop packing around the heaviness of guilt. You can run back to Jesus again, embracing and thanking Him for a forgiveness that is complete and defining. To truly follow Jesus in this brokenness of life is to be defined by Him. If Jesus isn't defining you, then something else is. For most people, that one thing is usually their performance.

So who defines you? Do you define you? Does your performance? Does Jesus define who you are? Maybe the best place to begin is to consider what you do when you fail and when you win. Are these experiences "defining" or simply part of our humanity? Who defines you?

Scripture for the Day:

Romans 4:22–25

Thought for the Day:

What does it mean to you that righteousness has been *credited to you?* What does this do to your focus on your performance? How does this help you with your struggle with sin and brokenness?

WORDS ARE POWERFUL

If you're old enough, you probably remember this phrase: "Sticks and stones may break my bones but names will never hurt me." I remember saying this back to a few classmates after some mean comment they hurled at me. I remember a few kids saying it back to me as well. Yes, I was on the giving end of more than my share of mean comments to others. But if this statement is true, why did we all still hurl the abuse? We continued because deep down we all knew it wasn't true. We all understood that words really do inflict pain … a lot of it. I can still remember words and how I felt when people said hurtful things to me in grade school. Sticks and stones can leave a mark, but those wounds will heal. The unfortunate thing about words is that they are so powerful, some people carry those wounds to this day. Words can create wounds that last decades and even a lifetime.

I am convinced this is why the Bible says so much about how we use our words. Words are such a gift to humanity. We have the power to build with our words or to destroy with them. Our words can hurt or heal. Words are profoundly powerful.

> Do not let any unwholesome talk come out of your mouths, but only what is helpful for building others up according to their needs, that it may benefit those who listen. (Eph. 4:29)

> If you bite and devour each other, watch out or you will be destroyed by each other. [We bite and devour each other by our words.] (Gal. 5:15)

It seems we live in a time when "biting and devouring" is the norm. Since this has become the standard for many people's behavior, so has the destroying. Marriages are being destroyed. Churches are being destroyed. Entire communities are being destroyed, all by the words being used. Even the gift of social media is often turned into a dark platform for verbal venom and malice with the intent to wound. Here is a tool that has the power to be used for good and the encouragement of many, yet often it is turned into a soapbox for personal attacks. As followers of Jesus, we must be different. We are light and salt in this world, according to Jesus. How can we embrace and walk in this role when our words sound no different from the world we are called to reach? If we say we are followers of Jesus, maybe one of the best places to start is following Jesus with our words.

Go back and think about what Ephesians 4:29 says to us. "Don't let *any* unwholesome talk come out of our mouths." Do you see how crazy different this is compared to the rest of the world? Can you understand how radical this is? Can you imagine how different this makes us look? Can we realize that one of the most observable indicators that people notice as followers of Jesus are the words we use … or don't use. We don't use our words to destroy people. Instead, we use our words for what is helpful, what builds others up, what is according to their needs. In other words, we use our words to serve others. We use our words to love others. We use our words to inspire others. Our words should build and elevate the people around us. They should never be used to destroy.

How are you using your words? If the only testimony you had for being a follower of Jesus was the conversation that you use, what type of witness would you have? Do your words set you apart? Are the people around you better because of the words you use? Do they feel loved, affirmed, encouraged, served, or supported? I know it's easy for us to think about the people around us and say, "They aren't talking to me like this either!" That may be true, but they aren't the ones reading this right now. You are. Jesus wants your relationship with Him to be defined not simply by your behavior but by the words you use. How do those words need to change?

How can you talk to your spouse differently? I'm sure we all need some growth on this one. How can you be more of an encourager to your kids? What about your neighbors or coworkers (yes, even the ones who annoy you)? What words can you use to build them up? What about your pastor at church? Maybe it's the ministry leader where your kids are involved. Some of these people rarely even get a thank-you from those they serve. Something as little as a word of appreciation goes a long way in people's lives, making them feel valued. Your words have tremendous power. Now go use them to make a difference in someone's life. Go follow Jesus with your words.

Scripture for the Day:

Colossians 3:5–17

Thought for the Day:

Spend some time asking Jesus whom He wants you to speak words to so you can build them up according to their need. Pray, asking that He would create in you a sensitive spirit to the people around you. Ask that He would give you the words they need to hear. Pray for the courage to do this.

DON'T QUIT MAKING A DIFFERENCE

Fall in the Pacific Northwest is a beautiful time. The leaves change as the days get shorter. The colors are vibrant and expressive. It's by far one of my favorite times to take a drive up in the hills above where I live and bask in the mosaic of colors created by the fall season. As gorgeous as this time can be, it's also messy. As the leaves turn, they fall off the trees into my yard, creating plenty of extra work. I have an abundance of oak and ash trees where I live. Keeping up with their weekly assault on my yard at times seems exhausting. Just yesterday I was out mowing my yard and sucking up all the leaves with my riding lawn mower. I love seeing my place after it's all mowed and picked up. It's just one of those simple feelings of accomplishment I enjoy. It takes about ninety minutes to mow my yard, and I was just about done when the wind suddenly picked up. Pretty soon the trees were swaying back and forth in a violent fashion. This went on for about an hour. Needless to say, it looked like it was snowing ... leaves! Ninety minutes of work down the drain. In a few short moments, you couldn't even tell I had mowed the yard. There was no feeling of accomplishment that day.

I think it's easy for us to feel this way about trying to make a difference in this life. The continual assault of evil on this world just seems so overwhelming at times. We can serve, volunteer, and throw ourselves into good, noble causes, but at the end of the day, the yard of this world still looks the same. It's still a mess. I know there have been times when I felt this way. In the moment it seems like we're making headway. It appears there is real and lasting change. We're encouraged as we look behind us at what was accomplished. Then there is that gust of evil that shows back up, and pretty soon it looks the same all over again despite our service and sacrifice. The winds of darkness blew the leaves back into the area we worked so hard to clear. Did it matter? Did it make a difference? Did it change anything? My answer is to all those who may be discouraged, and this is a resounding yes!

> Let us not become weary in doing good, for at the proper time we will reap a harvest if we do not give up. (Gal. 6:9)

> Therefore, my dear brothers and sisters, stand firm. Let nothing move you. Always give yourselves fully to the work of the Lord, because you know that your labor in the Lord isn't in vain. (1 Cor. 15:58)

Our efforts do matter. Our attempts at change and our desire to see transformation aren't in vain. I get the weariness part. I understand all too well the discouragement of hard work not appearing to pay off. Yeah, I've tasted that one firsthand plenty of times. I bet you have as well. Yet the word of God promises there is a harvest if we refuse to give up. There is a payoff, even if we don't see it today. It's worth it to teach those little kids in church. It's worth it to go on that mission trip. It's worth it to volunteer in that shelter or food pantry. It's worth it to volunteer and serve in whatever the Lord has given you a desire and passion to do. Why? Because Jesus says it matters, even if with your physical eyes you can't really see it. Some days when the winds of evil blow hard against our efforts for goodness, we must take it by faith that they matter and refuse to quit.

Yesterday, even after I was done mowing and my yard still looked horrible, it mattered that I was out there working. "Why?" you ask. When I put my lawn mower away, I walked through my yard, feeling a bit defeated, and stood at my compost pile. You see, this is where I put all my yard debris. The mound was about five feet tall; this was a testimony to all the leaves I had already picked up. Although my yard was a mess, there was quite an impressive pile of leaves that had been taken off my yard. Without my efforts, my yard would have been even worse, and the effort to pick all the leaves up would have tripled. This is true in life as well. Without our efforts, life would be so much worse, and the effort and energy necessary to make a difference would be multiplied.

If you've been feeling discouraged that you can't make a difference, maybe you need to get your eyes off the brokenness of this world and see all the leaves you've already picked up. Your efforts matter. Don't despair. This world is a better place because of you. It's not in vain. Jesus is proud of you, and someday He will show you the full extent of the impact you made in this fallen world. Until then, keep mowing.

Scripture for the Day:

2 Corinthians 4:8–18

Thought for the Day:

Where are you feeling discouraged that your efforts no longer matter? Is your lack of progress becoming a source of discouragement to you? Let me encourage you to take your eyes off the expected progress and find joy in what has already been done.

TO WHOM DO YOU BELONG?

Independence is wired into our fallen humanity. We exercised our self-will in the garden of Eden and rebelled against God; humanity has been on this course from that moment on. We don't like anyone telling us what to do. We want to do our own thing. As perfect and as adorable as my grandchildren are, yes, even they are very self-willed. Even at fourteen months, my innocent little granddaughter doesn't seem to appreciate the word *no*. I've even seen that angelic face scowl at me when I've had to redirect her behavior. She even threw a piece of toast at Grandma the other day. Oh, the horror! It is truly amazing how this independence is such an integral part of our humanity. We don't have to be very far from the womb before we begin exercising it.

"What's wrong with this?" you may ask. Everything! We were created for a relationship with God. We weren't created to live independently from Him. God didn't design us and then tell us to go live however we want. We were designed to live inside the context of a loving, obedient relationship with the One who made us. We don't belong to ourselves. We belong to Him.

Because this rebellion separated us from the God who loves us, God sent His Son to die on a cross to pay the penalty for our acts of independent rebellion and reconcile us back into a dependent relationship with Him. Now we can get back to the original design God intended. This is why Jesus said, "My sheep hear my voice; I know them and they follow Me." (John 20:27). We no longer follow ourselves. When we gave our lives to Jesus, we gave up that independence to live a life of dependence on the One who saved us. This is why the apostle Paul said, "Do you not know that your bodies are temples of the Holy Spirit, who is in you, whom you have received from God? *You are not your own*; you were bought at a price. Therefore, honor God with your bodies" (1 Cor. 6:19–20, emphasis added).

Until we come to this realization, our relationship with God will *never* work. Jesus didn't invade our lives only to be a resident, giving us eternal life someday. He comes to be Lord, Master, Savior, and Owner. We no longer have any rights to our lives. We gave them up to Him. Jesus now gets to have complete authority over our lives. He gets to call the shots. We live lives of humility and submission to Him. We take our cues from Him. We submit our wills, desires, and even aspirations to Him. We aren't our own. The blood of Jesus bought us out of the slavery of sin.

You see, independence is a myth. The truth is that we are slaves either to sin or to Jesus. We are servants either to this fallen world and this fallen kingdom or to Jesus and His kingdom. There is no third option. If you believe there is, you are falling for the same lie Adam and Eve fell for. You have never really been your own. Either Satan owns you, or Jesus owns you. Those are our only two options.

If you are a believer in Jesus and take great pride in "doing your own thing," let me caution you. Jesus died on a cross so you could have the freedom to do His thing. *Your thing* is a dead end. *Your thing* is part of the lie. *Your thing* cannot give you what your heart truly longs for. *Your thing* will eventually destroy you. True freedom and fulfillment are discovered in following Jesus alone. They are discovered in giving up one's self to Jesus to receive something much more priceless in return. Giving up control and following Jesus don't make us miserable. They are the only pathway to life.

Maybe today the greatest thing you can do to change your life is to humble yourself before God and give your life to Him. Don't just give Him your soul. Give Him your life ... all of it! Give Him all the jumbled, broken, ragged pieces you have been trying to manage. Hand Jesus the deed to your life. Get out of the driver's seat for once. Tell Jesus you belong to Him and Him alone. Make a choice to go from independence to dependence. What will this do? Everything! It's a choice that will finally make your faith in Jesus work. Why? Because you will be back where you belong. You are designed to belong to Him.

Scripture for the Day:

Luke 9:23–26

Thought for the Day:

Is Jesus simply *part* of your life, or is Jesus your life? Is Jesus merely a passenger in the vehicle who is along for the ride, or are you allowing Jesus to drive? Do you belong to yourself? Or does your lifestyle reflect that you truly belong to Jesus?

EPILOGUE

After Jesus' resurrection, He appeared to His disciples at various times before returning to heaven. One such time was at the shores of the Sea of Galilee. The group had fished all night and caught nothing. I'm sure they were all disgusted at the lack of fish in their nets. How do I know this? They were fishermen. All fishermen expect to catch something. Now they saw the silhouette of a lone figure standing in the dawn shadows. A voice called out and asked whether they had caught anything. They replied with one word. No. Then came this vaguely familiar statement: "Throw your nets on the right side of the boat, and you will find a catch." I'm sure they reluctantly did so, but as they found out, the net was so full of fish that they had to drag it to land. Now, this was their "lightbulb" moment. "It's the Lord! Jesus is here!"

Back on shore, Jesus had a fish breakfast waiting for them, roasting on the open fire. But it's the conversation with Peter, not the breakfast, that I want to focus on. After Jesus asked Peter three separate times whether he loved Him, there was a scene I believe has profound application for us.

John 21:20–22 says, "Peter turned and saw that the disciple whom Jesus loved was following them. [This was the one who had leaned back against Jesus at the supper and had said, "Lord, who is going to betray you?"] When Peter saw him, he asked, 'Lord, what about him?' Jesus answered, 'If I want him to remain alive until I return, what is that to you? You must follow me.'"

Peter asked about Jesus' best friend, John. Jesus quickly pointed out to Peter that Peter didn't need to know His will for John. Peter's focus wasn't John. His focus was to follow Jesus. "Don't get distracted thinking about what My will is for others. You follow Me, Peter!"

Sometimes during this journey of following Jesus, we can get our eyes and concerns where they don't need to be. We worry about the spiritual journey of others. We wonder whether they will follow Jesus as well. There is an appropriate level of concern, but it can also be distracting. Sometimes we worry about whether they will catch up with us. *Will they follow Jesus with me? What is God going to do in their lives? How is God going to use them?* Either way, we need to hear the voice of Jesus: "What is that to you? You must follow me."

As we have taken this journey together, may I encourage you to keep following Jesus, listening to His voice. You may ask, "What about the people around me? What about my family? What about my friends? What about my spouse?" They have to make the same decision to follow Jesus that you do. You can't make it for them. You can be salt and light, and fulfill your role as an ambassador. But you can't allow your concern for others hinder your wholehearted commitment to follow Jesus. "I'll follow You fully, Jesus, when my spouse gets saved." "I'll follow You with more fervor, Jesus, when my kids are out of school." "I'll be more committed, Jesus when …" I think you get the picture. Each one of us has an individual responsibility to heed the call of Jesus and follow. What if others don't come? "What is that to you? You must follow me."

I have been following Jesus now for over thirty years. There is a phrase I have used countless times. "Not everyone makes the journey." I have walked away from many people, ministry settings, friends, and opportunities so I could continue following Jesus. Sometimes these departures were mutual and blessed, recognizing God's call and hand. At other times, they have been extremely painful. At the end of the day, though, I am loyal to One. It has saddened me, as I have seen so many not make this journey, and yet I have experienced great joy with so many who have. Either way, I have to keep following Jesus. We haven't been called to simply have an intellectual belief system. We are called to hear the voice and follow the Lord Jesus. We follow a real, living, experiential Person.

My prayer is that this brief book has simply helped you to do just that. No matter who else you are following, may you keep following Jesus. Let me quote the old hymn "I Have Decided." One verse reads, "Though no one joins me, still I will follow." May those words reflect your commitment to Jesus, but may your reality be that many take this journey with you.

Scripture for the Day:

John 21

Thought for the Day:

Are you allowing your concern for others and their spiritual journey distract you from your wholehearted commitment to follow Jesus?

Printed in the United States
By Bookmasters